THE REVVED LIFE

ACTS 1:8

LIFE

FROM THE PITS TO THE PODIUM

Dear Amy and Girls!

Luv you guys!

Pardon Acts 20:24

THE REVVED LIFE

ACTS 1:8

FROM THE PITS TO THE PODIUM

Jeff Knight

FOREWORD BY ED YOUNG

REDEMPTION PRESS

Published by Redemption Press, PO Box 427, Enumclaw, WA 98022
Toll Free (844) 2REDEEM (273-3336)

Redemption Press is honored to present this title in partnership with the author. The views expressed or implied in this work are those of the author. Redemption Press provides our imprint seal representing design excellence, creative content and high quality production.

Editorial & Production Coordinator: Beth Neibert
Editors: Sally Reboul, Sam Severn
Cover Design: Tracy DeYoung

Released in the United States of America

ISBN 13: 978-1-63232-122-0 (SC)
          978-1-63232-123-7 (HC)
          978-1-63232-125-1 (ePub)
          978-1-63232-126-8 (Mobi)

Library of Congress Catalog Card Number: 2015937394

DEDICATION

To my beautiful, loving, spirit-filled wife, Melinda, and my vivacious daughter, Seven, for always being my biggest fans and exposing me to a life I never thought possible. Thank you, with my whole heart for my whole life.

To every friend, confidant, staffer, racer, crew and church member who has ever prayed for me, encouraged me, championed me, challenged me ... you are between the lines of every page. Thank you for being a part of my race of life. You make it special.

ACKNOWLEDGEMENTS

To Tracy DeYoung for creating a cover that represents going full throttle on the asphalt of life.

To Beth Neibert, Sally Reboul, and Sam Severn: you extend my hands, heart, and put a megaphone to my voice making this publication possible. I am speechlessly thankful. Your support is priceless.

CONTENTS

PART 3
The Profile of *The Revved Life*

PART 4
The Principles of *The Revved Life*

PART 5
The Theology of *The Revved Life*

PART 6

The Strategy For Living *The Revved Life*

FOREWORD
BY ED YOUNG

The first time I ever prayed what I call a "high risk prayer" I was 20 years old and a sophomore at Florida State University. Through a crazy set of circumstances, I received a full-ride scholarship to play basketball there. Up until that point my dreams centered on basketball. But, while I was at Florida State, a pastor challenged me to push my faith and pursue what God had in store for me.

So one night, after practice, I knelt down in my dorm room, rested my elbows on the air conditioning unit, looked out over a darkened parking lot, and said a prayer that absolutely changed the direction of my life. It wasn't a complicated prayer. It wasn't necessarily an eloquent prayer. But it was a genuine, heartfelt prayer and it changed everything.

I simply said, "God, help me to point someone to You tomorrow." That was it.

The next day, I was walking to class with one of my teammates. He was a guy who just transferred to Florida State from another school, because he'd gotten kicked off his basketball team due to drug usage. As the only Christian on the team, I was the one the coaches looked to as sort of a calming force on the team and in the lives of my teammates. So when the Florida State Seminoles picked this guy up, I did my best to help him. I never put my faith out there really, but I did my best to live the way God wanted me to live.

As we walked across the campus, we talked about all kinds of things, and I could tell something was heavy on his heart and life. All of a sudden he stopped, looked at me, and said, "Ed, there's something different about you, man. There's something you have that I don't. I don't know what it is, but I want what you have."

In that moment, I was absolutely ambushed by the power of God. I just felt His presence and I knew He was cracking open the door for me to walk through. So I began to talk to my teammate about my past, how I came into a relationship with Jesus, and what that meant in my life. I just simply told him my story. And God began to take over.

About five hours later I found myself in my friend's dorm room leading him in a prayer to commit his life to Christ. With tears streaming down his cheeks, I saw this guy step over the line of faith and become a believer.

That situation messed me up. My life has never been the same because of that transaction God allowed me to be a part of. What I experienced in that moment was the first real crank of God's engine in my life. It was then I began to understand what *The Revved Live* is all about.

The Revved Life is all about a life of high-risk prayers like the one I prayed years ago. It's about an impassioned pursuit of the things of God. It's about a life of reaching out to a lost and dying world.

But like any pursuit in life, we cannot just hope it happens. We can't just wish our way into making a difference. God doesn't want us to just wander through this one and only life. There are steps we must take, actions we must engage in, if we hope to make the most of what God has equipped us with.

Jeff Knight is all about faith in action. And he pours his heart and soul into every page of this book so that you, the reader, can learn to take the kinds of actions needed to in order to experience *The Revved Life.*

There are Christian leaders all across the world who, sadly, have mailed it in. They have become too comfortable in the La-Z-Boys of their faith. They have quit facing life head-on for God and left the hard work of reaching people to others. Jeff is not one of those leaders. It is clear through his story, his leadership, and his life he has a passion for Christ and a deep desire to empower you to live the same kind of life.

Be careful with the book you hold in your hands. This is a dangerous book. Why? Because it's going to change the way you live. While it won't provide you with a magic formula for your faith, it will motivate, encourage, challenge, and empower you to live the kind of life God has in store for you.

Remember, your faith isn't just about you. If it were, you would have been evacuated to heaven the moment you stepped over the line. No, it's not about you and it's not about me. The purpose of your faith is to reach other people—people who are in desperate need of a Savior. That Savior is Jesus Christ. And He is calling you to live the powerful life, the focused life, the eternity-altering life. In other words, Jesus is calling you to live *The Revved Life!*

—Ed Young
Founding and Senior Pastor, Fellowship Church
Author: *Outrageous, Contagious Joy,* and *High Definition Living*

ACT 1:
THE DILEMMA

I am a Christ-follower.
I could say I boldly follow Christ.
But really, sometimes I keep my faith private.
Really private.

For too long now, my delicate self-image has depended on people liking me.
I have tried with all my efforts to please people and win them over to my way.
Some have accepted.
Many watch from a distance.

I have used my voice to promote a lot of meaningless stuff: Hobbies, Companies, Products and Agendas.
Instead of following Christ, I've brokered Him.
Only looking for what's in it for me.
And when there's nothing.
I stop.
Engaging.
Sharing.
Listening.
Being.

And I've been emptied. And lost.

Every experience.
Every lesson.
Every encounter.
Every tragedy.
Every part of life.
Can become meaningful.
And purposeful.
As I reconnect with what God is calling me to do.

I'm getting back in touch with being a Christ-follower.
With the actual purpose of it.
Not the infection of popularity.
Or the virus of feeling important.
Or the obsession of, "What's in it for me."

I'm kicking my addictions to self.
And learning to follow Christ all over again.
This has been incredibly revealing.

I am finding that there are others.
Many.

Christ-followers everywhere are rediscovering Jesus. His words.
They are getting reacquainted with His final command: Reaching people far from God.
Not talking about it with friends.
Or writing about it on blogs.
Or simply "liking" it.
But … actually doing it.

It's what I've come to call *The Revved Life*.

INTRODUCTION: THE MAIN THING

've been a lead pastor now for fifteen years. Along the way, I've encountered many different kinds of churches.

Let me tell you, as a pastor, I love the church. I think every man and woman of God who serves, gives, and embodies the local church is a rock star.

And there is something I want to say to every single person in the local church. Something I think is absolutely necessary in these times. It's not an easy saying, so if this stings a bit I don't mean to offend.

What I mean to do is kick-start your faith again. Awaken the dormant dreamer within you and empower you to a bolder more risk-taking faith.

I mean to catalyze you to your original mission.

Here it goes ...

I've encountered churches that are devoted to community service. These churches feed the hungry and house the homeless. I've encountered churches that are devoted to political "justice." These churches promote social activism and work to improve society through political institutions. I've encountered churches devoted to religious ritual. These churches love pomp and ceremony, and they give rise to ornate cathedrals and impressive choirs. All are admirable, noble, and holy causes.

But these things don't reflect the *main thing* that Jesus came to do. They do not reflect the *main thing* that Jesus told us to do.

Jesus came to impart spiritual life, to redeem lost souls from the inevitable fate of a godless eternity, and He told us to be witnesses.

The *main thing* in God's sight is telling unbelievers (people far from God) about Jesus (winning souls), and then helping these new believers grow in their newfound faith (making disciples).

This is the *main thing*. Because Jesus made it the *main thing* before He left his followers and ascended into heaven.

Other pursuits may be good and noble. But everything else we could possibly do is secondary to the primary work of Christ.

Soul winning is the heart of Christ. So *soul winning* must be the heart of every Christ-follower, and every Christian church.

We must not allow anything else to deter us or distract us from our primary mission and responsibility.

We touch people's lives and we meet people's needs so we can have the opportunity to share Christ and to tell them about God's solution for their greatest need.

Here's an example:

If you feed a hungry child in Honduras, yet you never tell that child about the love of God and the forgiveness of sins through Jesus Christ, that child may overcome his nutritional problems and actually live a long and healthy life. But when he dies, he will enter eternity without Christ.

And if you help a drug addict kick her habit and make something good of her life, that young lady may become a great asset to society and live a long and prosperous life. But when she dies, she won't know the Lord.

So what good have you done?

What good is it if we pour ourselves into community service or political activism or religious ceremony, and yet forget the most important thing, the *main thing* that Jesus told us to do with our lives?

That's the heart of *The Revved Life*.

It's living out the *main thing* Jesus told us to do.

You okay?

Good, let's keep going.

The Revved Life is what I call living courageously for God.

The Revved Life is fearlessly facing life head-on.

The Revved Life is born out of passion. It is born out of the fire I feel burning inside me to elevate evangelism and soul winning to the forefront of Christian thought and attention.

It's high time we get more intentional.

More strategic.

More focused.

More excited.

About reaching a far-gone world!

I believe the church should assemble to celebrate the goodness of God and the power of God, and worship the Lord with intensity and study His Word with an insatiable appetite for spiritual knowledge.

But I also believe that the church should come out from behind the walls we've built up, and go out one-by-one to infiltrate every nook and cranny of our culture and society.

We should infuse every arena. We should navigate our way into every sector. We should pry our way into and penetrate every compartment, every aspect of human life, in order to touch people with the love of God, and then tell them about the plan of God for saving their souls and changing their lives.

Jesus said, "And what do you benefit if you gain the whole world but lose your own soul?" (Matthew 16:26, NLT).

There is nothing to be gained if we improve society, advance justice, and bolster the quality of life for those around us, only to neglect their souls and avoid confronting them with the uncomfortable truth ...

People are lost and in need of a Savior.

But that is precisely what Jesus told us to do.

In fact, He told us to make this task our highest priority.

He told us to make it the *main thing*.

SOUL WINNING

Because *soul winning* was the passion of Christ, it's disturbing the number of Christians who hide in churches and avoid humanity. I'm bothered by Christians who are forever studying, reading, and hoarding spiritual knowledge, yet never impart any of it to those who need it most.

The early church wasn't like this.

Sure, they were noted for being enthusiastic students of God's Word (see Acts 17:11, NLT). They were noted for their intimate camaraderie and their fervent prayers (see Acts 2:42, NLT).

But more than anything else, they were known for spreading their faith (see Acts 5:28, NLT), for unashamedly proclaiming the Gospel (see Acts 4:31, NLT), and for winning souls and planting churches (see Acts 19:10, NLT). In fact, every single chapter in the book of Acts has at least one reference to the resurrection of Christ.

Why? Because the resurrection of Christ was the heart and soul of the Gospel they proclaimed.

And that's the heart of *The Revved Life*. And that's the life I want you to commit to leading.

And that's the life that is not reserved for the spiritual elite.

Or the conservative pundit.

Or the right-wing Republican.

The Revved Life is available to everyone of us who have experienced the love of a living God, Jesus Christ! We matter. We have a sound. You and I have to raise our voices in this land. We have to tell the world!

So as you commit to *The Revved Life,* I want to share my own story.

I am going to tell you the story of my heritage, the story of my church, The Rock Church, and the story of how God taught me about winning souls by planting me in the most unlikely environment among the most unlikely people imaginable, so I could learn to showcase His love and proclaim His name in the most unlikely ways.

I will also share with you what I've learned about winning souls and, in the process, what I've learned about the Lord.

I hope *The Revved Life* will inform you.

I hope it will teach you something about God you don't already know.

But most of all, I hope *The Revved Life* will excite you about the possibilities of personally impacting people through your life, and glorifying Him by making a meaningful difference in the lives of those you encounter.

After all, that is the primary purpose for which God created you.

That is the return He hopes to realize for all He has invested in you.

And that is what I call, *The Revved Life*!

So fasten your seat belts and put your faith into overdrive, while I climb behind the wheel and take you on a high-octane ride to *The Revved Life*, right now!

PART 1

THE STORY OF *THE REVVED LIFE*

CHAPTER 1

MY JOURNEY TOWARD THE REVVED LIFE

Therefore, since we are surrounded by such a great cloud of witnesses, let us throw off everything that hinders and the sin that so easily entangles, and let us run with perseverance the race marked out for us.

—Hebrews 12:1, NIV

My father was a racer before he was a pastor.

My father taught me how to race before he taught me how to pray.

That wasn't an accident. And it wasn't a coincidence.

That was God's design.

As I begin this tale, the most important thing I've learned over the past fifteen years is that there's really no difference in God's mind between the "spiritual" and the "secular." We Christians tend to think of church as "holy," and work as "unholy." We tend to think of worshipping with other believers as "supernatural" while we think of golfing with our buddies as "natural."

We Christians have a habit of filling our schedules with "Christian approved" activities when in our hearts there is a gnawing sense something more exists for our life.

In our minds, we separate the two aspects of our lives—the spiritual stuff and the everyday stuff.

But God just doesn't see the world through that paradigm. He doesn't look at life that way.

So what is *The Revved Life*?

The Revved Life is lived by somebody who "gets it."

The Revved Life is lived by someone who has added Christ to his life, who is passionately pursuing God's best for his life, and who is consistently growing and improving in every aspect of his life, lifting others to new heights along with him.

He is prevailing in his struggles.

He is overcoming the obstacles that life has set before him.

And he is winning at life in general. He is winning people, as well, drawing them to himself and to the Lord through his words, his deeds, and his attitudes—but mostly through his involvement in the lives of those he touches and his willingness to come out of his hiding place to participate with these people in the events of their lives.

My journey toward *The Revved Life* began like so many others. A life-changing event ended life as I had known it, but became the entryway to an exciting new chapter.

It opened my heart to know God in a more fulfilling way, and opened my mind to a better understanding of my own purpose and destiny.

MY WAKE-UP CALL

It all began in the state of Washington on a cold, January evening in the year 2000.

My parents, who served as the lead pastors of our church, were on a flight, returning home from Puerto Vallarta, Mexico. They had been doing missionary work for the past several days. My wife, Melinda, who is the worship leader at our church, and I were in a recording studio in Seattle, where Melinda was cutting her very first worship album.

My mother Linda traveled to Puerto Vallarta almost two weeks earlier. She went there to preach and to personally attend to the mission she'd established. It's in one of the worst areas of the city. My mom was a strong believer and a powerful witness for Christ. Since she was saved as a young woman, she devoted herself to ministry and to building clean water wells near a massive garbage dump in Puerto Vallarta. That project was very close to her heart.

As often as she could, she would travel there to personally oversee the details of the operation, and encourage the pastors and local believers who joined in her work. Shortly before her scheduled return home, however, my father Joe flew down to join her.

It was their 32nd wedding anniversary, and he didn't want to be apart from her on that special occasion.

To appreciate what they were doing in Puerto Vallarta, and why they were there, you'd have to know some things about my parents.

You see, Joe and Linda Knight were amazing people. Simple folks, they started life just like many other young couples, working and trying to get by. After my father got out of the Air Force, he worked as a contractor and as a radio ad salesman before he entered the ministry. He also owned a motorcycle shop where he sold and serviced them. My mom worked for the State of Washington, as part of a team of social workers, helping people with drug and alcohol addictions get clean and sober.

They were good people. They loved me and my little sister Jenny very much, and they always gave their hearts and souls to everything they put their hands to.

My parents delighted in the simple pleasures of life, especially in the people who were close to them. They didn't "jet-set" around the country, hobnobbing with the rich and famous.

Nor did they pursue affluence or notoriety.

Instead, my father spent his early years riding and working on motorcycles, getting just as dirty as a man can get. And my mother, an avid horsewoman, spent her time riding and showing horses.

Before my parents were saved, and I was between the age of three and seven years old, my dad would compete in motorcycle races practically every weekend. And I'd go watch him. I also remember my grandparents, aunts and uncles, and our family friends going to the track to watch my father race. And later on, after my dad gave up motorcycle racing, he would still take me to the track to watch the auto races.

I loved watching my dad race motocross. Later in life, after he stopped racing, I would look into his competitive eyes as we'd watch the car races. He made me want to be like him. He was larger than life to me. And to this day, motorcycles or car races, it doesn't matter, are still what I watch the most.

Nearly 40 years later you will still find large quantities of Motocross, Supercross, and NASCAR™ on my DVR at home.

When I was a kid my parents turned everything into a family event and "people time."

In fact, I learned my ABC's and how to count to 100 at the racetrack.

So you see, my dad introduced me to the world of racing long before the Lord called me to be a pastor ... a little "clue" to the shape of my destiny.

THE BIRTH OF THE ROCK CHURCH

Then on the night of June 3, 1978, both my parents met Jesus.

They were in two different places that night—my mom at home and my dad in jail for a crime he'd committed—when each gave their hearts to the Lord at the same exact time, without either one knowing it was also happening to the other, and without ever hearing the Gospel.

It was an absolutely miraculous, sovereign act of God and one that I'll share more details about later in my story.

After that day, all their passion and all their energy were suddenly focused on Christ. Everything else quickly became subordinate to their primary passion, the pursuit of the Lord.

This passion led them to start a small Bible study in their house.

And because my mom and dad were so passionate about God's Word and so energetic when it came to their relationship with Him, this little Bible study group quickly grew into a small congregation.

And then that small congregation evolved into a great church.

And suddenly and quite unexpectedly, my parents found themselves as the lead pastors of Cornerstone Christian Center, in the town of Woodinville, which would later become The Rock Church.

Neither of them had any ministry experience, or any formal theological training. But they had come to know Jesus, and both knew how to be bold in their faith.

They were able to believe God for anything, and they were willing to approach anyone, anywhere, to tell them about the glory of the Lord.

In the beginning, it was their childlike passion for Christ and their uninhibited ability to trust and share the message with others, which became the invisible pillars of their fledgling church.

It was this same boldness and confidence that caused that little congregation to grow until ministry became my parents' singular focus, and their full-time occupations.

In fact, the actual birth of The Rock Church could really be traced back to the miracle God worked to transform both of my parents, that night he brought them to a spiritual U-turn that altered the direction of their lives.

That's why my mom was in Puerto Vallarta, to follow God's calling. And that's why my dad joined her there for their 32nd wedding anniversary.

They wanted to celebrate together while serving the Lord.

They wanted to make a difference.

They wanted to leave a mark and a legacy for Christ.

They had already built a great church. Now they wanted to touch the nations and impact souls everywhere. They wanted to preach the Gospel and show the love of Christ to hurting people. And they wanted to be in the company of other believers in different parts of the world who were serving the same great God and fulfilling the same Great Commission.

But their work in Puerto Vallarta ended that day, and they were both on their way home to me and my sister Jenny, who was 16 at the time.

And as that cold January day progressed and the time drew near for their plane to land in Seattle, I received a phone call at the recording studio in Seattle.

A close friend from the church told me that there had been a terrible airline crash, and that a plane went down in the Pacific Ocean, about 11 miles off the shores of Southern California. So I rushed to the little television set they had at the studio and moved the rabbit ears around so I could get a picture from the local ABC station.

As I looked through the fuzzy picture at the helicopter hovering over the blue water and floating debris, the TV announcer repeated the flight number: Alaska Airlines Flight 261. My heart stopped. My dad's personal assistant Rachel happened to be with Melinda and me at the studio that day, so I looked at her and asked, "Is that my parents' flight number?"

She was pale as she answered me. "It is, Jeff."

There was this long silence. Melinda's eyes met mine—I could almost see the wheels turning in both of our heads, as we both rejected the awful possibilities. In my mind I thought: *Survivors. There have to be some survivors.*

And as the night progressed, we eventually learned that all 88 people on board Alaska Airlines Flight 261 died when the plane suffered a catastrophic mechanical failure, and plunged into the ocean below.

HOW GOD USES EVIL FOR GOOD

No words can describe how I felt. I was devastated.

At the time, I was a young man, just 29 years old. My life would never be the same. My father and mother were my closest friends. They were my mentors and my spiritual guides. Since the day I was born, they made me a part of every aspect of their lives. And since the age of 7, the name of Jesus was on their lips and resonated in our home.

They were my heroes in so many ways.

And they were my inspiration for the future.

But now they were gone forever. Both of them!

After the initial shock wore off, and I started thinking again, I realized that the death of my parents affected a lot more people than just me. After all, they were pastors of a growing church, and pillars in our community. They had many friends, protégés, and everyday people who looked to them as spiritual shepherds and teachers.

What would these people do?

Where would they go?

What would their lives look like from now on?

What would become of our church?

Those were the questions that rattled around in my brain, for days and weeks afterward.

The days following the crash were frightening and uncertain, because the only thing I knew for sure is that nothing would ever be the same—for me or anyone else I knew.

But then God began to reveal His plan.

He began to show me how He was going to create something beautiful out of something devastating.

How He was going to use this tragedy to perpetuate my parents' legacy and actually build upon it.

How He was going to take something the enemy intended for evil, and turn it into something that God could use for good.

On the Tuesday night after the crash, the other members of The Rock Church gathered at my parent's home with Melinda and me. On that occasion, one of my father's board members approached us.

"Your Dad always talked about handing you the church one day, Jeff," he said. "The Board believes that time is now."

I looked at him with bloodshot eyes, on the verge of tears, and I gave him a nod of affirmation. And with that, Melinda and I became the lead pastors of The Rock Church, following in the footsteps and carrying on the legacy of my father and mother.

For fifteen years, Joe Knight labored to build that spiritual house and to establish a strong Gospel witness in our community.

Now, in the blink of an eye, it was my turn to assume that responsibility.

So on the very next Sunday, February 6, 2000, I stepped into the pulpit to preach my first sermon as the lead pastor of The Rock Church.

CHAPTER 2

INSIDE THE CATCH FENCE

But that life-changing series of events was just the first half of God's amazing plan to bring beauty out of the ashes of destruction, and to take my life and our church in a whole new direction.

He didn't just call my father and mother home to be with Him, and then set me in my father's place. He also providentially reconnected me with a good friend from my past, named Mike. Together, Mike, Melinda, and I took The Rock Church in a brand new direction, which no one could have foreseen or prepared.

Growing up, Mike and I spent a lot of time together. But you know how things go. As he and I got older, we migrated into different social groups. Then we chose different career paths, and over time, we just drifted apart. After high school, he became a racecar driver; I pursued a career in ministry. We both continued to live in the Seattle area.

Then one day, Mike saw a billboard advertisement for The Rock Church. So he decided to give me a call.

I was so surprised to hear from him. We chatted for a few minutes, before he told me the reason he called.

See, Mike was the driver for a team that participated in the Whelen All American Series of NASCAR™. Most people are familiar with the

Sprint Cup Series that involves the top drivers on the top NASCAR™ tracks on Sunday afternoons. But not too many people know that NASCAR™ has tentacles that reach into smaller communities all over the country. They sponsor different kinds of races on different kinds of tracks with different kinds of cars, and they do this virtually everywhere.

Mike was part of the program that conducted Saturday night races at local tracks in our area. The races were 30 to 200 laps and held on tracks that ranged from one-quarter mile to five-eighths of a mile in length.

And, like any automobile racer, he was looking for sponsors for his team. Stock car racing is an extremely expensive sport.

So that day, Mike asked if I would like to sponsor his racecar.

He said I could display any type of legal advertisement I wanted on the front, sides, and back of the car. And I could change the advertising anytime I liked. I have to admit, it sounded interesting. And it would certainly be a creative way to let people know about The Rock Church.

Ask yourself: how many churches do that kind of advertising? That kind of publicity could really set us apart, and make our church stand out! It could also give us some much-needed exposure with the locals, the people we were desperately trying to reach.

The Evergreen Speedway was in the same town as The Rock Church, not far from where I grew up.

So I told Mike I would think about his proposition.

And the more I thought about it, the more the idea appealed to me.

It was really different.

I bounced the idea off some of the key people at church. But it didn't go very far. Getting involved in auto racing seemed a bit too radical for them. Besides, the church had a limited advertising budget. So I just dropped the idea.

But the idea continued to gnaw at me. Finally, Melinda and I decided to get involved on a personal level. We'd recently sold a piece of property, and had some extra money to invest. So after much prayer, we made the decision to take the plunge. I called my friend Mike to ask if it would be possible for me to be a bigger part of his team than merely a silent sponsor. That's when I discovered that his partner was looking to sell his portion of the team.

And that's when he offered me the opportunity to buy his partner's share.

I jumped at it.

I went into this partnership with boyish excitement, thinking this would be a wonderful opportunity. I'd have a new hobby and an escape from some of the stress associated with ministry. Plus I'd be hanging out with other men on the weekends, doing things men like to do. Awesome!

I mean, what red-blooded American male doesn't like cars?

To me, this was a double-barrel winner: I could have something to do to relax and unwind, and the church could get some free publicity in the process.

But I didn't know anything about the racing world. Absolutely zero! I had no idea how that world worked, or what it was like on the inside of the catch fence (the barrier that separates the people in the stands from the racers on the track and the mechanics in the pit area).

As it turned out, knowing absolutely zero was the right path for me.

Knowing absolutely zero about my path helped prepare me for the mission God had for me.

RACING FOR GOD

Thinking back on that pivotal decision, and the naïve excitement I felt about injecting myself into the strange new world of racing, I'm reminded that you just never know which events are going to turn out to be watershed moments in your life.

You know what I'm talking about, right?

Most of the things we do on a daily basis are things that just come and go.

They're part of our lives for a while, then the routine responsibilities of life take us in a different direction, and those things disappear as quickly as they'd arrived.

But every once in a while, there's a seemingly insignificant event in a person's life that becomes a critical moment in his destiny.

Partnering in a racecar was that event for me. Because this little advent into advertising became the doorway that God cracked wide open to take my life in a whole new direction, and to catapult our church toward its ultimate reason-for-being.

But before I tell you what started to happen I need you to know there was something instinctive, almost primal, about this venture. It was like I was reacquainting with a long lost friend. It was as if I was looking through a time machine into my past.

And it was answering a huge question.

Or maybe it was an inner need.

At any rate, it was exactly what the Lord had designed.

Feeling these early emotions of being involved with racing at a high level, like my father before me, had a redemptive component to it. It was as if the Lord was connecting me with my father's past, but without the crazy life that ended him up in jail.

Remember how I told you my dad found himself in jail the night he gave his life to Jesus? And how my mom also prayed the same night?

Well, it was a Friday, and I had just gotten home from school. I was seven years old. I'd been riding my dirt bike around the field most of the afternoon. My mom approached me about planning my birthday party. It was a month out, so I was like "cool." We planned on making it a party like none other!

But I learned later, the party planning was just a distraction. My dad was being jailed for nine counts of theft and two counts of forgery. White-collar crimes, not being honest with his taxes, and stuff like that; but the backlash of those poor choices put him on a collision course with Jesus Christ.

Both finding Christ and being in jail changed my dad. Certainly, and I wouldn't understand it until much later in my life, my dad meeting Jesus as his personal Lord and Savior, changed my destiny. But, at first, I saw something much different.

My Dad quit racing. I mean just *quit*. Gave away his race bikes. He sold his tools. In fact, he would seldom help me ride my bike any longer.

But I never let go of wanting to race. In fact, my new partner in racing, Mike, and I rode dirt bikes for a class project in the 9th grade. And, even though Dad wouldn't be anywhere near a motocross track, my uncles Jim and Jack and my grandpa Joe would load me up and take me around the NW to compete in different events.

But I longed for my Dad.

I wanted his blessing to race.

Instead, he coached my soccer, basketball, and baseball teams. We had soccer goals in our backyard, hoops around the driveway, and even a batting cage along the house with a pitching machine. Daily, my buddies would be present and we'd be working on our skills, depending on the season and sport we were playing.

Dad was totally devoted and I loved him for it!

And … I wanted to race. But racing wasn't in the plan of my youth, but, as an adult, things would change.

And time would be redeemed.

And the Lord would open a child-like desire only He knew I had.

The racer was being born, again.

MY FIRST DAY

I'll never forget my first day at the racetrack.

I was invited to the Evergreen Speedway to attend my first race as the part owner of a NASCAR™ race team!

For the first time in my life, I was going to be able to buy a pit pass, and go into the pit area with my driver, my team, and the other owners. I didn't know squat about the mechanical operations of a racecar. And Lord knows I wasn't qualified to drive. But I could still be involved.

I could help clean the car.

I could wax the car.

And I could put the decals and stickers on the car.

And the little boy in me was really excited about that.

So, on the morning of that initial race, I attended an event at the church, and then I hustled over to the speedway for the first practice session. I was so excited! I was wearing my special Rock Church team T-shirt. I had The Rock Church autograph cards ready. And I was feeling really high as I watched that beautiful Chevrolet Monte Carlo SS fly around the track with The Rock Church logo all over the hood and the sides of the car.

The car looked awesome as it chewed up the track. I was stoked beyond belief to see The Rock Church and God so gloriously represented and I was absolutely "revved up" and ready to go!

As I approached the pit area where our team was stationed, our driver was just coming off the track. He'd been doing the initial laps to test out the car. And you can just imagine the excitement of that scene. As soon as a driver pulls into the pits, organized chaos ensues. And it's exhilarating to watch. Every guy there knows his job, and he jumps right into it.

One guy takes tire temperatures.

Another guy jacks up the car.

Another guy measures air pressure in the tires to see how the temperatures are affecting the tire pressure.

Another guy records all the data.

And still another guy takes down the window net and interacts with the driver.

Everywhere you look, there's the buzz of excitement and things are happening. You feel the adrenalin rush through your body as you watch these skilled artisans tackle their tasks with amazing speed.

Then the driver climbs out and tells the crew chief what's right with the car, and what's wrong with it.

But as the driver climbed out of the Rock Church Monte Carlo and took off his helmet, I had a moment—an "epiphany," if you will—that gave me serious pause.

You see, the driver began to explain to the crew chief the problems he was having with the car.

And as he started listing the functions of the car that weren't working properly, the conversation among some of the crewmembers got really heated, and passionate... to say the least.

You see, in professional racing, the automobile is the key. The driver is important, of course, and a good crew is essential. But the car is the key.

If the car isn't working perfectly, you have no chance of winning the race.

The difference between first and second place in a professional stock car race often comes down to a fraction of a second. So the littlest things matter, and the goal of every team member is to make sure that each operation of the car is absolutely perfect. In fact, the primary focus of those practice laps is to get the car as close to perfect as possible.

The engine.

The handling.

The suspension.

The tire pressure.

Everything has to be completely flawless on that automobile! And while the practice laps reveal the imperfections, the job of the crew chief is to make the automobile right.

But apparently, the car was far from perfect that morning. And I could sense the frustration some of the crewmembers were experiencing. As they talked and put their heads together to figure out a solution, one of the guys got pretty exasperated.

Eventually his language got quite "colorful," as he let the others know how irritated he really was.

F-bombs were dropping.

Now let's get something straight here. I'm a big boy.

I may be a pastor of a church, but I can handle the real world. I don't live in fantasyland and I wasn't raised in a monastery.

There's nothing anyone could say that I hadn't heard a thousand times before. Besides, I knew when I got involved in this venture that the guys at the track wouldn't behave like the guys in my church.

I didn't expect them to.

But the scene I witnessed that morning served to remind me I had crossed a significant cultural barrier.

And I'd have to decide which side of the catch fence God was leading me to stand on.

Was I going to play it safe and sit in the stands, letting other people do what the Lord was asking of me? Or was I going to stay on pit road and figure out how to navigate what I was feeling?

CHAPTER 3

HEADING TOWARDS A COLLISION COURSE

That day at the track, I stood there wondering if I was up to the challenge of living with one foot in the church world and one foot in the racing world.

The guys on the team were great, and I felt privileged to be there with them. I also had no doubt that some of them would eventually become lifelong friends. So they didn't offend me or make me question my commitment to the decision I had made.

But a few of them were really rough around the edges. And I was wondering what my church members might think of me for spending most of my free time with these guys.

More importantly, I wondered what the community might think of my church, seeing the contradictions between what seems to be "Christian approved" in the community and the coarse nature of some of the guys associated with our racing team.

So as the conflict between my two worlds became clearer to me, I felt a little bit like a fish out of water.

I mean, I must admit that I was captivated by all the excitement and activity, and enthralled by all the sights, sounds, and technical stuff going on around me at lightning speed.

But now a big dose of reality had slapped me in the face.

I was suddenly forced to deal with the fact that I was about to put myself in the line of fire by trying to walk the tightrope between two competing cultures.

Luckily, everybody was busy doing what they do. So nobody was really paying much attention to me. Eventually, the driver climbed back in his car and went back on the track for some additional laps.

But when he pulled the car into the pits again a few minutes later, the same guys in the crew got in another discussion.

Harsh words were hurled.

The F-bomb flew again.

That's when something came over me.

I don't know what it was, but I rose to the occasion. I don't even know why I was so motivated to confront the struggle. Looking back years later, having been at the track now for nearly 15 years, I wouldn't be the least bit phased by the language or the scenario that was unfolding; I would simply live *The Revved Life* anyway.

But I think God was pulling me out from under the shelter I'd been living beneath.

I was a passionate Christ-follower.

I had been immersed in Christian culture since college.

And God used this situation as the catalyst to awaken my soul that He wanted me to relocate. He wanted me out from behind the pulpit of a church service, so He hurled me smack dab in the middle of real men who were racing cars.

I had a whole gamut of feelings. I wished to remain ignorant. But something would not let me. The Lord was asking me.

Calling me.

And it made me nervous.

Fears of not belonging invaded my mind.

I was under tension.

The whole thing stood me up to take notice. Something within me was awakening. It was hard to put my thoughts in order, but I eventually did.

I gained the nerve.

I rehearsed my thoughts.

And just went for it.

I pulled aside one of the members of the team.

"Look," I said, "I may be a pastor, but I *can* handle all this intensity. I need you to understand you can't use the F-bomb anymore. I need you to understand that you're representing The Rock Church, the church on the side of our car. And I want our church to be proud of everything we do while people are watching us."

The guy just stared at me and blinked, like somebody awakening from a long sleep.

And after my heart rate subsided and I realized I wasn't going to be kicked to the curb, we carried on with a great day of racing.

Years later, I would learn that moment was pivotal in that guy's life. But as I stood there on that first day at the track, trembling with an adrenalin overload, I suddenly realized that I was standing at a crossroads in my life.

I was on a collision-course.

A place where my Christian beliefs and all my Christian experiences would collide with a mindset that was as far removed from the church world as anything I had ever committed to.

I couldn't just pull the plug. I was too invested. Financially.

Not to mention these guys had become my friends. I wanted to be there.

I wanted to race!

There was really only one choice.

And it was at that moment I firmly decided that I was supposed to be a pastor.

But I also was supposed to be a part of a great race team.

So, standing on that spot, I made up my mind to merge my two worlds.

I knew it would take years to be accepted into the racing community. And I knew it would take years to earn their trust and to make inroads into their lives.

But that was the day I decided to start the journey. And God quickly confirmed for me that this was His will for my life and my ministry.

HUMBLED

Since then, God has continued to confirm the decision I made that day by granting me the joy and satisfaction of watching a lot of spiritual fruit emerge from the soil as a result of stepping onto that racetrack.

And now, years later, I can look over my congregation and Facebook friends and see the faces of many men, women, and children who came to Christ because I decided to get uncomfortable and to cross the invisible barrier between the church world and the outside world.

For instance:

Easter Sunday 2009, I was humbled looking out over my congregation to see eight of my peers—eight fellow drivers from the racetrack—worshipping the Lord with us that day.

Some of them were champion drivers, race winners, or winners from other divisions of NASCAR™.

I had spent time with each of those men. I had talked with them and nurtured relationships with them. I personally prayed with six of them as they invited Christ to become the centerpiece of their lives.

And now they were seated in my church, worshipping God with me and celebrating the resurrection of Christ.

The following year, on Easter Sunday, my friend John raised his hand at the end of the service and invited Jesus to be Lord of his life.

Now, let me tell you this about John. He had been a fierce competitor of mine on the racetrack for years. But after battling with our team for the trophy week after week, he finally visited The Rock Church for the very first time on Palm Sunday 2010.

He then returned on Easter Sunday with his girlfriend Stephanie, and the two of them prayed with me to accept the gift of eternal life.

John was water baptized the very next Sunday. Since then, he and Stephanie have married, and John and I have become good friends.

He's served as my crew chief, and is involved in our church as much as racing allows him.

And he is ablaze with passion for the Lord.

Another man I would meet was Chris, a racecar driver from Canada. Chris owned a restaurant in British Columbia, and one day while at work, he was severely injured in a terrible explosion. In fact, Chris was burned so seriously he was not expected to live.

Several days after the accident, I drove up to Canada to visit Chris in the hospital burn unit. To this day, I can vividly recall the nauseating smell of burnt flesh that permeated the hospital ward. But after forcing myself to enter the room where Chris was lying in a coma, his entire body wrapped in gauze, I did the only thing I knew to do.

I prayed the best prayer of faith that I could pray.

And I asked God to heal him.

As I stood there, I noticed that some of the gauze on Chris' left hand had come loose. I was able to clearly see the charred webbing of the skin between his fingers. It bore witness to the critical nature of his wounds, and I knew that if God did not perform a miracle, Chris would never drive again, much less survive.

But God's shown me repeatedly through my life that He does perform miracles.

And two years later, I was sitting on the pole position of a race, with Chris on the outside position revving his engine right beside me. He raced me hard that day, neck and neck, all the way to the finish line.

During the annual awards banquet at the end of that racing season, Chris was voted "Most Inspirational" by his fellow drivers and crew chiefs. The track management asked me to present the award to him. To a standing ovation, Chris accepted the award that night, and God received the glory as His ability to heal was confirmed in a powerful way to a crowd of blown-away people.

CHAPTER 4

UNCHARTED TERRITORY

The message of that evening—the message that God heals—is the message I was destined to live and to proclaim in the NASCAR™ culture.

God heals broken bodies.

But He also heals broken lives, broken hearts, broken dreams, and broken relationships. And the past fourteen years have proven this to me, time and time again.

Nevertheless, I stood there that first day on the track, gripped with the realization that I was brashly forging into uncharted territory.

It slammed into me that I would be colliding head-on with all these future relationships, and all these future opportunities to minister to people.

To share the Gospel.

And to impact lives that hung in the balance.

I guess I could have done the easy thing, that day. The safe thing, the thing that would have brought me the cheers and accolades from the Christians who believe in playing it safe and keeping a healthy distance between themselves and "sinners."

But I just couldn't do that.

Once all the arguments and quarrels subsided, our race team ended up getting the car in good shape for the race that night. But just before the main event, the track officials decided to conduct a "trophy dash," something they do to entertain the fans and to build excitement for the main race.

A "trophy dash" is a short race of about six laps, involving the top four qualifiers for the main race. The winner gets an extra purse—some extra prize money—and a small trophy.

Our team was selected to start on the pole position. Our driver put the pedal to the metal and got off to a great start, and he held the lead all the way to the checkered flag.

The Rock Church had brought home a trophy.

How cool is that!

A NEW TYPE OF MINISTRY

The truth is, I got into racing for the fun of it.

I wanted to race.

I felt like it was an opportunity to meet a side of my dad I didn't know.

I never really thought about the ministry aspects of what I was doing.

I got involved with racing so I could have a hobby, to meet some new people and have something to do with other men that could give me a break from the pressures of my work.

But I quickly realized that this venture was not going to be a break from ministry; it was going to be a new *type* of ministry.

I realized that I had stumbled my way into a whole new world of people who would never darken the doors of a church—yet who needed Christ as much as anyone.

People that God loved!

People that God wanted in His family!

People for whom Christ died!

People with whom I would spend the majority of my time—and people who would challenge me in the years to come in every imaginable way!

In the pages that follow, I want to share more of my story, the story of how I merged ministry with racing. And, how God managed to build a tremendous and exciting church in the process.

It's the story of how a church full of people opened their eyes to a new way of looking at lost souls, and at new ways of reaching them.

And I want to share the story of how God reached my mom and dad, in two completely different places, at exactly the same time.

But for now, let me just say that I eventually made the transition from racecar owner to driver, and spend many Saturdays now racing in pursuit of a checkered flag.

But I also continue to serve as lead pastor of The Rock Church. Today, there are dozens of people sitting in our pews who never knew Christ before I showed up at the track. Today these precious men and women of God serve as ushers, teachers, board members, and worshippers in our church.

But I had to reach out beyond the walls of the church, to reach these people.

I had to inject myself into a world and a subculture that was as far removed from my comfort zone as I could possibly get.

And I had to step into a world where people had no idea that Christ existed in a way they could connect with.

INSIDE *THE REVVED LIFE*

I want you to see how my undertaking into a new arena helped start the process of leading people to Christ.

I want to take you inside The Rock Church, a building full of people facing their fears head-on, people living *The Revved Life* and raising up more leaders for the Kingdom of God.

I want to take you onto the track with me, and beyond the catch fence into that unique subculture of American life, so you can see how one committed Christian can make a difference and leave a mark on the world.

I want to open your eyes to a new way of looking at people.

I want you to learn to see people the way Jesus saw them, when He traveled the countryside.

And I want you to learn to approach them the way Jesus approached them, when He introduced Himself into their lives and interacted with them where they lived and worked.

I want you to see the sights and smell the smells that are still part of my racing weekends, and I want you to feel the feelings that I have felt since venturing into this unusual place of ministry.

But most importantly, I also want you to learn the Biblical principles for *The Revved Life*—principles I have learned from my own hard-knock experiences—principles that have made my life complete and have turned my church upside down.

To God, it's all about touching people's lives and restoring them to Him. He wants to meet that individual right where he is and make his life a million times better than he ever thought it could be.

God doesn't look with favor on the church attendee while despising the mechanic.

God doesn't love the follower and hate the fallen plumber.

God loves all people equally. And He wants each man and each woman to become everything He created them to be.

He wants us to be saved. He wants us to be whole. He wants us to have purpose and significance.

And He wants abundant life for every individual.

So why do Christians huddle in churches, with all the saved people, and stay far, far away from the lost racecar driver or the backsliding racing fan just down the street?

Why do we immerse ourselves in Christian books, podcasts, and worship CDs, while the people at the track remain lost and without hope because we avoid them?

Jesus spent as much time in the streets and in the homes of outright sinners as He did in the synagogues or the homes of the so-called righteous. Yet we insist on spending all our time with those who think like we think, and who behave as we behave.

But how does that help the lost man at the racetrack? And how does that fulfill the most important command that Jesus ever gave—the command to share the Gospel, and to make disciples?

How does that build the church?

Guess what.

It *doesn't*.

Hanging out at church with all your church buddies might be the safest way to live. But nobody ever did anything great by playing it safe.

GOD HAS A RACER'S HEART

The more time I spend at the racetrack, the more I'm convinced that it was God's providence that led me there, and it's God's plan to keep me there.

In fact, I've come to realize that God has a racecar driver's heart.

It's true! I don't know what He thinks about NASCAR™ per se, but I do know He has an awful lot to say in the Bible about racing, and about those who compete in races.

He likes them both.

We see racing chariots as early as the second chapter of the little book of Nahum (see Nahum 2:4, NLT). And in the New Testament, the apostle Paul and the writer of Hebrews used the analogy of racing to help the early believers learn basic principles about personal conduct, spiritual determination, self-discipline, and eternal reward (see 1 Corinthians 9:24-27; Galatians 2:2, 5:7; Philippians 2:14-15; Hebrews 12:1-3, NLT).

What's more, my experience on the racetrack has helped me fulfill my destiny in life and in God's work.

Had I listened to the conventional wisdom of the typical Christian, I probably would never have volunteered beyond the predictable role of an evangelical minister, and I probably would never have been able to lead my church into the excitement we now know as unorthodox soul winners and people living on the edge of faith.

But now that I look back on things, I know this was always God's plan for my life.

It just took God's intervention to help me see how to blend the two aspects of my destiny in order to do with my life what God wanted me to do all along.

And what did God want me to do?

He wanted me to be a pastor.

But He also wanted me to be a racer.

And He wanted me to take my faith with me into both arenas: into the racing world where unbelievers would become followers of Jesus Christ, and then into the church world where those new believers would become productive members of the body of Christ.

CHAPTER 5

JESUS TAKES THE POLE POSITION

What is your passion?

What is your all-consuming motivation in life?

What is that "thing" that drives your internal engines and makes your heart leap within you?

I don't know what your passion is. Only you can discover that.

But as I share more of my story, and the life-changing principles that God has taught me through this amazing adventure, I want you to realize that you, too, have a destiny in the Lord. Even though God is the foundation, and the church is the centerpiece, there is an element of your destiny that is unique to you and that separates you from everyone else.

God has given you a specific calling in life.

And He's given you a specific set of gifts and talents that were designed to equip you for that calling.

But be warned: Giving Jesus the pole position in your life will often take you places you don't want to go.

Jesus isn't a GPS you can stick on the dashboard and expect to be guided on the easiest possible route to your destination.

Your destiny may take you into an arena of life that your Christian brothers and sisters can't share with you, because they don't understand that world or have a passion for it.

God didn't seek you, save you, change you, and fill you with all the knowledge you've gained about Him so you could huddle with other like-minded people inside your church or cower inside your prayer closet while those outside die and perish in a Christ-less eternity.

That's not *The Revved Life*!

God did what He did so He could prepare you to infiltrate a segment of the world where you and you alone can share things you have seen and heard.

You are God's point of entry into a slice of society that nobody else can reach.

You are His connection with a subculture of unbelieving souls who are as distant from God as they can be—yet who are more open to the Gospel and hungrier for spiritual truth than you could possibly imagine.

You'll be amazed at how impactful your life can be, and how persuasive your testimony can be, if you'll only share it.

You'll also be amazed at how faithful God's support will be when you live *The Revved Life* in your assigned place of spiritual service.

MOTIVATED TO PRESS TOWARD THE FINISH LINE

Listen, God doesn't make mistakes. He knows what He's doing. And everything He's ever done in your life has an eternal purpose and a redemptive rationale.

Your job is to realize it.

Discover it.

Embrace it.

And then figure out how to use it to bring glory to Him.

God used Paul's Roman citizenship to set him before Felix, Festus, Agrippa, and Caesar.

God used Moses' position as the adopted son of Pharaoh's daughter to give him access to the throne room of Egypt.

God used David's experience with the harp and the sling to provide him a seat at King Saul's dinner table.

And God used Esther's beauty to give her influence with King Xerxes.

Everything in your life that was BC (before Christ) has a purpose in your life AD (after deliverance).

Every experience, every talent, every relationship, every expertise—God wants you to use your knowledge and experiences to make a difference for Him in your unique corner of the world!

He wants you to infiltrate that dark space of Satan's empire where other Christians fear to tread, and where he keeps multitudes of souls in spiritual chains because no one dared to enter and shine His light.

God has destined you to be a light in the darkness.

He has destined you to be a thorn in the side of unbelieving men.

He has destined you to be a voice, an eyewitness, and a beacon of hope for those who have no hope.

Just think about it! Is the world getting closer to God or farther away?

It's a no-brainer—the world is getting farther away from God. And why is that? Is the church on the offensive or the defensive? We're on the defensive. We are retreating to our conference centers and our sanctuaries, our retreat centers and our Christian-only cruises.

We are staying as far away from the "sinners and tax collectors" as possible, because we want to be separate and holy.

And we want to be comfortable.

But what happens when we abandon government and retreat inside our churches to hide?

What happens when we abandon public education and retreat into our conference centers to hide?

What happens when we abandon the music industry, the entertainment industry, business, public policy, and even auto racing, while we retreat into our sanctuaries to huddle with one another in our cushioned pews?

I'll tell you what happens: The godly grow *weaker* and the ungodly grow *stronger*.

The godly *decrease* in number and the ungodly *increase* in number. The godly *surrender* control of every aspect of daily life and the ungodly *take* control of every aspect of daily life. The godly become *irrelevant* and the ungodly become *relevant*.

Are you getting the point?

If we fail to obey Jesus by willfully infusing ourselves into every corner of society and every aspect of human life, we surrender the souls of lost men to the enemy. We abdicate our assigned role as the stewards of God's creation. And we fail to achieve our primary purpose in this world.

We are here to do what Christ told us to do.

And it's time for us to realize that the lost souls won't come to us; we must follow the example of Jesus.

And *meet them where they are.*

I believe that Christians should go to church whenever the people of God assemble. We need the fellowship. We need the corporate worship. We need the prayers of our leaders, the encouragement of each other, and the instruction in the Word of God. We need to be lifted up when we are spiritually weak, and we need to be exhorted for the Christian journey, which can be uphill at times into the headwinds of adversity.

But we also need to realize that the primary purpose for assembling is to be equipped for service (see Ephesians 4:11-12, NLT).

We are there to acquire the tools we need to take Jesus with us into that little corner of the outside world where nobody else can go.

He wants us to be His eyes and His ears in that place.

He wants us to be His hands and His heart. He wants us to do His work.

He wants us to sense the needs around us.

And He wants us to be His voice, to testify for Him where no one else will speak on His behalf.

So let's take this journey together.

Let's press toward the finish line.

We're not that different, you and I.

What I've experienced on the racetrack is probably similar to what you experience in your workplace, or among your friends and family every day.

And what I have battled at the racetrack is probably similar to what you've battled as you've sought understanding about how to merge your faith with your everyday life, and how to "fit in" with your friends and coworkers while "standing out" as a witness for Christ.

I want to share my crashes and my last-place finishes as well as my victories with you.

I want to share my story, and a lifetime of insights that have guided me toward living *The Revved Life.*

Your job will be to take *The Revved Life* in and apply it to your life.

I know God will help you.

Press on, until we each win our race, and receive the heavenly prize for which God through Jesus Christ is calling us.

Now let's get ready to pop the clutch and drop the hammer on the next part of *The Revved Life*!

PART 2

THE HEART OF *THE* *REVVED* *LIFE*

CHAPTER 6

A HEART TO WIN

Do you not know that in a race all the runners run, but only one gets the prize? Run in such a way as to get the prize.
—1 Corinthians 9:24, NIV

God flipped a switch inside me, the first time I heard that verse.

It's one of Apostle Paul's boldest messages.

It's one of God's greatest slam-dunks, if you ask me.

In the comparisons he drew between racing and the Christian life, Paul defined what the heart of *The Revved Life* should look like.

Paul compared the man racing around the track for a prize, and the believer being driven through life by a purpose.

Paul made it clear:

Not only is racing a noble and admirable pursuit, but it provides us with a perspective on life that's the same as God's.

If you want to see God's view of running the race of life, just head out to your local racetrack.

I still remember the months that followed my first day at the track. Those months proved to be a pivotal time for The Rock Church.

As I began to spend more time at Monroe's Evergreen Speedway, I started to see the impact we'd have as a church long-term. It began to matter we were there. Not necessarily the racing aspect of it all. That was fun for sure, but we were making friends. We were gaining inroads with the fans, other racers, and officials.

And I was able to see what God could accomplish when one person dared to take the words of Jesus seriously, climb behind the wheel of a race car, and do something bold for the Lord.

Our team raced six times that first season. The guys on the crew did a great job, putting us in a position to win each time we hit the track.

In addition to winning the trophy dash early in the season, we put the car on the podium two other times finishing 2nd and 3rd. We were gaining legitimacy as a race team sponsor, too.

Even on the nights where we didn't fare as well. There are so many variables at the race track to eliminate your pursuit of the prize. And, even though a racer can encounter engine failure, crashes, or flat tires, there's really nothing to dampen the spirit after racing gets in your blood. It was in my blood since I was a boy - just a few weeks into my new adventure. It was awesome!

Looking back I realized one thing about that first season. I had aligned with a really good team. We were always running in the top 5. My driver and his key crew members were not beginners. They were seasoned veterans with multiple wins under their belts, and they'd teach me a lot about racing in the coming years.

In addition to performing well on the track we were impacting lives with our racing, we also saw God do miraculous work in our community, on one of our nation's darkest days.

It was the Sunday following 9/11. A terrifying time for America and a Sunday unlike any I'd ever seen as a pastor. Everyone I saw that day was starving for hope.

On that following Sunday when we were all desperately seeking stability, optimism, and a sense of meaning to our lives, several of the men from the racing team showed up with their families at The Rock Church, for the very first time. They all sat together, and seeing them there as I spoke from the pulpit literally gave me goose bumps.

I felt a spiritual awakening that day.

I experienced an intense connection with my own purpose.

It was one of the highlights of my life.

Now you might recall those were highly emotionally charged times, back in 2001. But by the end of the service, some of those members from my racing team walked the aisle to meet me, and together we prayed. Jesus met them. They met Him. It was a collision of awesomeness.

You want to talk about exhilarating moments?

A walk-off homerun moment for God. And for me.

It was clear. God had me in the right place at the right time.

Don't get me wrong. I still faced scary, uncharted waters every time I took my faith out to the racetrack. But after that, I began to see the results from my visits to the racetrack. More and more people from the speedway started coming to church. And eventually, almost every member of my crew ended up giving his life to Jesus Christ.

Ka-boom! This is why I am alive: The Revved Life.

So I thank God I didn't decide to stay safe in my little pastor's box.

The adrenaline-pumping thrill I felt as I watched God riding shotgun in these other men's lives could never have happened, if I had given up after the first string of F-bombs were launched at the track.

Should I have quit? Should I have caved in, after that first day?

Some would say, "SURE! PROBABLY!" But not me. There's **no quit** in *The Revved Life.*

Instead of backing down I felt driven to share my faith with a new audience, one that was hungry for hope. And after taking that risk for God, God took the wheel and did the rest.

God was adding to our impact rapidly—The Rock Church was growing—and a big part of it was because of our unorthodox involvement in the racing world.

It was because God had shown me the heart of *The Revved Life,* and then put my foot on the gas.

I learned in a breathtaking way that racing is a beautiful metaphor for life and for Christian service.

And that's how we began closing deals and winning souls for Christ. Living *The Revved Life*.

RACE TO WIN

The heart of *The Revved Life* is racing to win.

Remember that verse from Paul I quoted earlier?

Paul also wrote:

"Everyone who competes in the games goes into strict training. They do it to get a crown that will not last, but we do it to get a crown that will last forever. Therefore, I do not run like someone running aimlessly; I do not fight like a boxer beating the air. No, I strike a blow to my body and make it my slave so that after I have preached to others, I myself will not be disqualified for the prize" (1 Corinthians 9:24-27, NIV).

See, God understands how life works.

In fact, God created life.

So not only does God accept the competitive nature of life, He approves of it.

He wants us to compete! He wants us to bring everything we have to the table—our courage, our creativity, our grit and our resilience—and then race to win.

That's why He encourages His children to do everything they do with excellence.

He wants us to do our best in school.

In business.

In marriage.

In parenting.

He wants nothing but our best when it comes to financial management.

He wants us to unleash our best when representing Him nobly before an observant world.

God wants us to win! He wants us to win at life!

To have winning homes, winning personal relationships, and winning businesses!

He even wants us to take the checkered flag at the racetrack, if that's your thing.

Winning is where we all want to be. It's the best. It's exciting.

And it's hard!

If there's a disservice been paid to the young people of the world it's the "participation award." We need to clearly teach our kids that participation is not winning. Winning is winning. And winning is hard. I think Paul is imploring us to know the difference because when we distinguish between the participating and winning we can learn invaluable lessons about life.

God taught me such a great lesson about *The Revved Life* a few years ago.

This was back in 2010. I was driving in the Washington 500. The car was running awesome that day. I'd been fortunate to lead most of the early laps of the race, and I had the feeling we'd be putting the #70 car in the winner's circle.

About midway through, I had a setback, and fell to the rear of the pack. Eventually, however, I worked my way back to the top of the leader-board after the first-place driver blew a tire.

But shortly after reclaiming the lead, my friend John climbed from the middle of the pack to challenge me for the position.

Lap after lap the two of us stayed tight in the turns, John's car right on my back bumper, ducking underneath to the bottom of the track as I held the high line, hoping for a chance to pass on a corner, in an epic battle, a neck-and-neck race to the finish line.

As I came out of the number 4 turn and the flagman lowered the white flag, marking the final lap of the race, I made a critical mistake and John grabbed the lead. I scrambled to catch up but he gunned it and sailed around the track all the way to the finish line, claiming the win.

I was blown away. On one hand I was good enough that day to win. On the other hand a mistake cost me dearly. I lost.

As we stood on the podium after the race to receive our trophies for first and second place, my victorious buddy John took the microphone from the master of ceremonies and publicly honored me as his pastor, mentor, and friend. But as he held the first-place trophy high for all to see, he turned to me and said:

"I hated beating you. But if you didn't get my best effort, I knew you wouldn't be satisfied to win."

He was *absolutely right!*

King Solomon, widely recognized as the wisest man who ever lived, wrote about subjects of excellence and personal performance.

He said: "Whatever your hand finds to do, do it with all your might" (Ecclesiastes 9:10, NIV).

God wants your boldness to shine brightly.

He wants you to be tenacious.

Tireless.

Rock-solid, when you run your race.

He's prepared you to do great things on His behalf. And when He opens the gateway to future success, He wants to see you blast through and hit the ground running with all your might.

But God is not pleased when He gives you the capacity to imagine great things—

To endure great challenges—

To complete great endeavors—

And to climb impossible mountains—

Only to see you hold back and settle for less—just so you won't surpass the person running beside you.

If God gave you the talent, He wants you to use it.

To hone it.

Sharpen it.

Perfect it.

He wants you to give Him your best. To squeeze the most out of yourself that you can possibly squeeze.

And if that means second place is the best you can do …

Awesome!

So be it!

But if that means you can take first place, that's okay, too.

The Revved Life has taught me this principle: *Race to win. Live to win.* The hard knocks and mistakes I've faced have turned this principle into my life's default setting. And ministry (including soul winning) has reinforced it in my heart.

I must run the race of life with the intention of winning. Stock car racing has helped me to understand this better, and to appreciate how it operates in my own life and in the plan of God for His people.

To do less than your best is to fail the Lord in the name of a false and self-serving humility.

WINNING REQUIRES TRUST

There's one thing you should understand about the race of life Paul mentions in his writings. It is paramount in the heart of someone ascribing to *The Revved Life*.

You can't win at life without the right equipment, the right support, and the right people. You've got to trust all these things.

Now let me make that even clearer:

You can't win without the whole armor of God.

And you can't win without God's help and assistance.

A victorious life is the result of a collaborative effort between you, the Lord, and the people God has placed in your life to encourage you and to assist in your pursuits.

One of the great lessons I learned early in my racing career was the importance of trusting my "spotter."

A spotter is a guy who sits above the stands, where he has a clear view of the entire track, and communicates with his driver by means of a wireless communication system.

I don't use mirrors in my racecar. I don't even have them. I find them distracting. When I start focusing on what's happening behind me, I can't concentrate on what's happening in front of me, and I end up losing focus and speed.

But occasionally it's necessary for a driver to know what's going on behind him, and who's sneaking up to challenge him for his position.

That's where a driver's spotter becomes invaluable.

The driver's helmet is equipped with headphones and a microphone, so he's able to talk to his spotter. He's also able to listen to his spotter, receiving specific instructions for the race. The spotter keeps the driver informed of what's going on behind him, and the spotter gives the driver much-needed advice and directives regarding the way he should run the race.

This is a fantastic example of how believers should run the race of life.

A racer must have great people surrounding them. So will you as you live *The Revved Life.*

We should always run to win.

But no person can win without God's help.

God can see things we can't see.

He knows things we can't know.

So, in the same way a rookie driver must learn to hear his spotter's voice in the midst of all the noise and confusion of the racetrack, the believer must learn to hear God's voice in the midst of all the confusion and chaos of life.

In the same way a rookie driver must learn to depend on another's guidance, the believer must learn to function by looking ahead to God's plan for his life, not behind him at his past mistakes.

And in the same way a rookie driver must learn to trust the things his spotter is telling him about the race, the believer must learn to trust those things the Lord is telling him about his life and his pursuits. Even though he can't see them for himself.

When a driver learns to transition from street driving to track driving, and when he learns to trust his spotter instead of mirrors, he'll have greater success in running a good race and winning the prize.

When a believer learns to hear God's voice, and learns to trust God's voice when he hears it, he can win the prize that God gives to the believer who meets the Lord's expectations for his life.

Run the race of life *well.*

And run it to *win.*

Live *The Revved Life.*

CHAPTER 7

A HEART UNAFRAID OF PURPOSE

Fear is a terrible thing.

Fear is the enemy of purpose.

Fear is a destroyer of destiny.

And God has a destiny and a purpose for each of his sons and daughters.

Do you have a vision of your purpose? Your destiny? How you can use the gifts God gave you, and put those gifts into maximum overdrive?

Few ministers have ever had a vision as compelling and powerful as the one that drove the Apostle Paul.

Paul was a former Pharisee. He persecuted Christians, threw them in jail, and hunted down and murdered followers of Christ. Before his name was changed to Paul, he was known as Saul of Tarsus. But while traveling one day to Damascus searching for Christ-followers to execute, Saul met the resurrected Messiah on the road.

That meeting radically changed Saul. It compelled him to change his name, indicating the new life he would lead from that point forward. Paul would devote his life to the pursuit of the mission Jesus would give him after his conversion.

Jesus communicated with Paul through a man named Ananias. And God told Ananias that Paul would become his "chosen instrument to carry my name before the Gentiles and their kings and before the people of Israel" (Acts 9:15, NIV). So this mandate from God became Paul's motivation for the remainder of his earthly life.

This heavenly directive became Paul's marching orders.

His driving force.

His passion.

His vision.

And his dream.

Paul also realized he was not a lone wolf in his service to the Lord, but rather one member of a great family of believers.

He had to lift up his eyes from the place where he'd once been, to see the place God wanted to take him.

He had to overcome his fears, and surrender to God's plan.

"I wanted to make sure that we were in agreement," Paul later wrote to his fellow believers in Galatia, "for fear that all my efforts had been wasted, and I was running the race for nothing."

God has a destiny and a purpose for your life.

And even though your destiny will be unique to you, your destiny will overlap with mine and with the destinies of other believers.

God has given you talents and abilities that He has not given to me.

Those talents and abilities are in sync with your destiny.

And, as soon as you buckle up your faith and strap on those God-given talents, He will assign you to work for Him in a corner of the world where your talents can best be utilized for His glory.

But even though our destinies are unique, there will be similarities between your destiny and mine.

For one thing, God will want us to attract people to Him in our respective fields of labor. Just as He assigned Paul to carry His name and build disciples among the Gentiles and the Israelites, He has assigned me to win souls and build disciples among those in the racing world.

And you'll be expected to do the same thing in your unique place in the world.

But how can you be successful in the pursuit of your destiny, unless you know what your destiny is?

Without a clearly defined purpose, you'll never be as effective for the Lord as you could be with a strong vision.

Paul was focused on his vision. He knew his purpose in life. He wasn't willing to let anyone or anything distract him from that purpose.

I'm focused on my vision. I know my purpose, and I'm not willing to let anyone or anything move me from my purpose.

You also need to know your purpose, and where God intends to *plant* you.

A man without purpose can certainly go to heaven.

But a man without purpose can never be as effective for the Lord as a man with a clearly defined vision.

Vacillation and uncertainty, therefore, are the enemies of your destiny.

And the other great enemy of destiny is fear.

That is why Paul wanted to submit his ministry message and ministry plans to Peter and James for their input and approval. He wanted to eliminate all fear and all indecisiveness from his life and his work.

He wanted to make sure that the plans for his life were benefitting the church and not conflicting with it.

Paul's purpose benefited the church. He refused to be in conflict with the Kingdom.

This is a great indicator for a believer. Purposelessness cannot exist in the life of a believer. *The Revved Life* may not know every nook and cranny of his or her purpose, but it knows the ingredients.

People.

Jesus.

Church.

Mission.

Hope.

There may be others, but that's a great start.

TWINS: FAITH AND FEAR

In Hebrews 11:1, KJV, we read God's definition of faith. According to the Lord, faith is "the substance of things hoped for, the evidence of things not seen."

But fear is precisely the same thing.

Fear is "the substance of things hoped for, the evidence of things not seen."

Faith and fear are two exhaust pipes on the same engine. Both operate exactly the same way.

Faith is the ability to accept something as fact before it can be proven.

Fear, also, is the ability to accept something as fact before it can be proven.

Faith is the belief that a certain thing is going to happen, a belief so strong and so convincing that it can enable a person to live his life as if that thing has already occurred.

Fear is exactly the same thing! It's the belief that a certain thing will happen, so strong and so convincingly that it can enable a person to live his life as if that thing has already occurred.

The only difference between faith and fear are the objects of their focus.

While faith focuses on God and on the good things He has promised, fear focuses on past experiences and disappointments and on the potential for those things to occur again in the future.

But Paul didn't want fear to be his motivation in life. Paul didn't want to live defensively, guarding himself from the possibility of making a mistake with his future.

Instead, Paul wanted to live purposefully.

He wanted to confirm his chosen path with the leaders of the church so he could put his fears aside and strengthen his resolve for the work that was ahead of him.

That's why Paul used the analogy of a race to explain why he went to Jerusalem. Paul was saying that life itself is a race, and that no man can run that race well unless he has a clear objective in mind.

For the NASCAR™ driver, the clear objective is the checkered flag and the winner's circle.

For Paul, the clear objectives were the Gentiles, their kings and the people of Israel.

The clear objective for *The Revved Life* is representing Christ through the way you live. That's the best way to introduce Him to the people who are in your circle of life.

Here's another way of looking at it:

Paul could not confidently pursue his life's work until he first addressed his fear of doing the wrong things. The NASCAR™ driver cannot confidently pursue his purpose on the racetrack until he also addresses the fears that are naturally associated with racing cars at triple-digit speeds.

Likewise, a person living *The Revved Life* cannot pursue his purpose in life until he confronts the fears that often stifle him in his efforts to live for Christ, to win souls to Christ, and to speak for Christ in an environment that is not conducive to faith.

Fears like:

Being afraid of confrontation.

Being afraid of failure.

Being afraid you aren't good enough.

Aren't fast enough.

Smart enough.

Until you face these fears and triumph over them, your potential as a witness won't be maximized. The power you could unleash to be a witness for Christ will be like a souped-up racecar with only a few drops of gas in the tank.

Limited.

Pastor and best-selling author Jentezen Franklin said, "When faced with fear, I have a choice. I can draw back or I can press forward and let my faith fight the fear."

This is true in racing.

This is true in life.

And this is true in *The Revved Life*.

Faith and fear may have the same definition, but they're not compatible and they can't coexist in the same heart. To live a *Revved Life* therefore, a man or woman of God must learn to confront fear and to run their appointed race with purpose.

They must reject their doubts, pick up the dream that's eluded them, and press forward.

They must grab the wheel of their true destiny, and pursue *The Revved Life*.

Just like Paul did.

UNDETERRED PURPOSE

You were running the race so well. Who has held you back from following the truth? It certainly isn't God, for he is the one who called you to freedom.
—Galatians 5:7-8, NLT

Let's think about Paul's question to the Galatians here for a moment.

Think about what has held you back from pursuing the life God put you here to lead.

Can you see it? Good!

Now let's address the issue Paul was talking about here.

The issue is faith.

Faith is what allows us to surrender our lives to the King, to our Lord, to Jesus Christ.

Faith erases doubts.

Faith obliterates mistrust.

Faith choke-holds fear.

Faith fires us with fuel to run the race.

Faith is what fuels our desire to run the trail God's blazed for us and to run it *well*.

Remember how I said the heart of *The Revved Life* is to race to win? Running with undeterred purpose is the fuel.

Running with undeterred purpose is the flame that feeds *The Revved Life*.

But how do we kick-start that flame?

What's the first step out of the starting gate?

You surrender your old self-worshipping nature.

You surrender your spiritual defeats.

Your past losses.

Your disappointments.

Your mistakes.

Your failures.

You surrender by closing the door to all those old stumbling blocks that have made you halfhearted, lukewarm, and held you back.

And you surrender your heart and life to Jesus.

Again if needed.

Make no mistake about one thing:

Jesus didn't set the pace when He began his journey to save souls only to hold back on the throttle.

Jesus was not given to mediocrity.

He was sold out to excellence.

In everything He did, He did it *with undeterred purpose*.

And this is a reflection of the nature of God seen throughout the Bible.

For instance:

When God created the universe, everything was *very good* (Genesis 1:31, NLT).

And when God led King Solomon to build a temple for Him in Jerusalem, it was *magnificent* (1 Kings 8:13, NIV).

See, God doesn't do things halfway, and He doesn't do things sloppily. God does everything with purpose.

He does it *undeterred*.

Since you're created in the image of God, and you're God's ambassador in the place where He's planted you, then you should strive to do everything *with purpose*. Why?

Because you're God's representative!

You're on His street team!

You've got the name of His Son carved on your heart!

If you're a believer, you'll be able to enter the presence of God for eternity.

If you think about it that's a pretty sweet deal.

But if you want to hear those beautiful words all believers long to hear when they get to Heaven, *"WELL DONE, good and faithful servant"* (Matthew 25:23, NKJV)—then you're going to have to do one more thing.

You're going to have to represent the Lord *well* and run your race *with undeterred purpose* while you're here on Earth.

Let me share the story of my friends Fred and Jaylene with you.

Fred and Jaylene are awesome people. When I first met Fred and Jaylene, they weren't believers. But today they've been part of The Rock Church family because of an opportunity that God presented to me at the racetrack.

You see nine or ten years ago, I was at the track, watching our driver run some practice laps. Fred was there, too. He's a fellow driver in the Whelen All American Series. He'd just brought out his brand new car and was putting it to the test during some practice laps. Fred and his crew had worked hard all winter long on this new car in order to get it ready for the upcoming season, and now the time had finally come to put the pedal down and see what this car could actually do.

I remember watching Fred that day. I really didn't know him personally. We were acquaintances, nothing more. We'd raced against each other. But that day I was watching Fred because I was impressed with his beautiful black car. See, Fred is an auto body repairman. He can paint anything, so his car was a gorgeously sculpted racing machine, built for maximum performance, with the final goal of doing one thing and one thing only: *Winning!*

As I stood there, watching Fred circle the track, I noticed he went into turn 1 a little deep. He began struggling to maintain control as he came out of turn 2 and blasted onto the backstretch.

Now sometimes a driver can save himself in those situations. Sometimes he can't.

Unfortunately, Fred couldn't quite regain control, and he ended up—BOOM!—crashing that beautiful, brand new, black car into the fence in front of turn 3, tearing the nose completely off.

I watched Fred bring the car back to the pit area on the hook (the tow truck) to see if his crew could repair it and get it ready for the race that night. It seemed that a part on the rear end of the car had failed, causing him to lose control and drive into the fence. It happens. And the part couldn't be repaired; it had to be completely replaced before the car could be taken back onto the track.

I watched Fred slumped on the hood of the car as he sat there with his head hung.

My heart really went out to Fred. I know firsthand the work it takes to prepare these cars, so I was really feeling for him. It just so happened that my team had an extra one of those parts he needed in my pit box, so even though it might later cost us the race, we gave it to him anyway.

Little did I know that this seemingly insignificant gesture would give rise to a great, long-term relationship.

It wasn't but a few weeks later Fred and Jaylene showed up at church for the very first time.

And it wasn't long after that Fred gave his heart to the Lord. Since then, Fred and Jaylene have served the Lord, and their children have, too.

Fred doesn't race much anymore, he's retired. But when he did, the two of us had some awesome battles on the track. We'd put our heads down and absolutely go at each other. Truth is, we had a lot of fun doing it. Now Fred and his entire family are serving the Lord, and he and I have a mutually rewarding friendship. We've experienced an amazing spiritual turnaround through our relationship with Christ and motor sports. In fact, Fred often tells people, "I get close to my pastor door to door, coming off turn four."

Fred and my connection over a failed racecar part is a splendid example of seizing the opportunities God sets before us in the place of ministry He has assigned us.

Mine is the racetrack. It's the asphalt track and the banked turns, the pits, and the high-velocity thunder of cars blasting to the finish line that gets me pumped.

That's where God planted me to run with undeterred purpose.

Running your race with this kind of focus, doing the right thing with the right attitude for the right reason always glorifies God and produces good spiritual fruit.

No matter where God plants you, do all that you do with purpose.

And do it in a way that invites the Lord to get actively involved in what you are doing.

CHAPTER 8

A HEART
OF DIGNITY

T hose who follow Christ have a goal in mind.

We like to *win*.

But winning isn't winning if you don't do it right. If you don't earn it, it's not worth having.

And if you don't win it with dignity, it's not going to fulfill you or bring the Lord honor.

We are encouraged to let others see our good works and glorify our Father in heaven. I love winning because it makes my Dad look good!

The Apostle Paul recognized this to be true. He told the believers in Philippi:

"Do everything without grumbling or arguing, so that you may become blameless and pure, 'children of God without fault in a warped and crooked generation.' Then you will shine among them like stars in the sky as you hold firmly to the Word of Life. And then I will be able to boast on the day of Christ that I did not run or labor in vain" (Philippians 2:14-16, NIV).

Isn't this an amazing passage?

What Paul's saying is this: It's okay to be proud of yourself! It's okay to take satisfaction in what you do, as long as you do it right and as long as you do it well.

This is not the evil kind of pride that flows from haughtiness, or an unrealistic opinion of yourself. This is the good kind of pride. Like the way you feel at the end of a long day when you look back and see the results of a hard day's work.

And God wants us to feel this kind of pride. He wants us to have a sense of accomplishment and a sense of purpose. He wants us to have significance in our lives, and He wants us to realize that we matter.

That our lives count.

He wants us to know that we are His children.

We aren't worthless.

We aren't useless.

No way!

We have value—and each of us has an important contribution to make to Him and to others.

God's children are special to Him. Paul realized this about himself. You need to realize it too.

DIFFICULT PEOPLE

When you're doing what God has called you to do with your life, do you ever encounter difficult people along the way?

Man, I certainly do!

I'm sure you encounter the same thing, when you try to live for the Lord and represent Him in your life.

Remember that people who don't know the Lord don't have anything better to live for than themselves. For them, first place isn't about doing their best.

It's not about unlocking their best potential.

It's about one thing:

Beating you!

It's about getting their names in the paper and their faces on TV. They want the bright lights, the fame, the glory, the money, and the opportunities for advancement that come with a showcase full of trophies.

The child of God who has a healthy opinion of himself isn't looking for the glory.

He's going to honor the Lord.

He wins because he lived up to the very essence God put within him in the first place.

For the one living *The Revved Life,* it's not about dominating another human being to gloat and draw attention to self. *The Revved Life* gives attention to the Father. It doesn't say, "Wow, look at me!" Instead it exclaims, "Look at Him!"

The Revved Life honors God and the potential placed within the one daring to put it on the line.

And that same person is going to take pride in what he does. He's going to work hard to make sure his life has purpose, and that his work has value.

He's going to work hard to do everything he does with excellence, so he can be proud of his achievements and take satisfaction in knowing that God is pleased with his life.

The man or woman who runs the race of life with dignity is the person who will leave a mark on the world.

They will make a difference.

They will impact people for Christ, and impart a legacy of wisdom, love, grace, and a sense of the awesome presence of God.

So run to *win!*

And work hard to be the best you can be!

Compete against the best that God has placed within you, seeking every day to do a little better than you did the day before.

Seek to excel!

In your life.

In your work.

In your finances.

In your relationships.

And even in your hobbies.

Demonstrate your skills and your drive for excellence in all that you do.

But most importantly, seek to do all these things with the mind of Christ, no matter how your competitors and teammates may behave.

So you can be honorable and bring glory to the Lord.

CHAPTER 9

A HEART TO FINISH

Never give in. Never give in. Never, never, never, never—in nothing great or small, large or petty, never give in except to convictions of honor and good sense.

—Winston Churchill

Racing has taught me one hardcore truth, one life-changing thing that a lot of people never get from real life.

Maybe you've heard it yourself:

There is a goal to everything worth doing.

For the NASCAR™ driver, that goal is the finish line, where the checkered flag is waved and the victor is named.

But life has a finish line, too.

And when the race of life finally ends, you'll be rewarded accordingly.

If you've completed your course, you'll be rewarded.

If you've exceeded expectations, you'll be rewarded.

If you've overcome great obstacles to place higher on the leaderboard than others thought you could, you'll be rewarded.

And if you've handled yourself with dignity throughout the race, you'll be rewarded.

But the race will eventually end, the points will eventually be tallied, and the results will eventually be made official.

So run your race with this in mind.

ETCHED IN STONE

Once again, the Apostle Paul understood this principle better than anyone, and he used the analogy of racing to help the Christians at Philippi understand it, too.

"I press on to reach the end of the race," Paul wrote, "and receive the heavenly prize for which God, through Christ Jesus, is calling us" (Philippians 3:14, NLT).

Now I'll be honest—anytime Paul's talking about racing, I'm a guy who takes his words seriously.

What Paul's saying is this:

The race will end when it ends.

And when it ends, the results will be forever etched in stone.

So make the most of your race while you're still running. And never stop pressing toward the prize that is waiting for you at the finish line.

Never take your eyes off the trophy, which is the approval of the Lord, and the crown of righteousness that is laid up for you in heaven.

ONE FOOT SHORT OF THE GOAL

Not quitting is right in the wheelhouse of what *The Revved Life* stands for.

Let me say that another way:

You don't have to necessarily be the best or the greatest to win the race.

You don't have to be the fastest.

Or the strongest.

The bravest.

Or the smartest.

You don't have to be the most experienced, the most ambitious, the most skilled or the most schooled, to win the race or to place high in the standings.

You can win the race, simply by *refusing to quit.*

Don't quit!

Too many Christians stop short of the finish line.

They give up too early.

They pack it in, when hardship and tragedy and trouble start breathing down their necks.

They quit.

Have you ever seen someone with *a quitter's mentality?*

A *quitter's mentality* is all about expecting defeat. About being overmatched by life. It's not about overcoming obstacles, or climbing out of the pit you're stuck in, or fighting to the finish.

We have a lot of *quitter's mentality* going around in today's world of ultra-convenience and effortless results. "If something gets too hard or if it takes longer than you thought it would, just quit," we hear. "After all, your happiness is the most important thing and your personal comfort trumps everything else."

So people are conditioned to give up and to quit the race just one foot short of the finish line.

But God doesn't want us to quit.

Ever!

My friend Dr. Dave Martin preaches at The Rock Church occasionally. Dave's written an awesome book, titled *The Twelve Traits of the Greats* (Harrison House Publishing). In his book, Dave devotes an entire chapter to persistence.

According to Dave, persistence is one of the twelve traits of highly successful people. And in his chapter on persistence, Dave tells a true story about a young woman from rural Alabama, named Edith.

Now Edith grew up during the Great Depression in a remote area of the state. Because of the simple life she lived, she never had the opportunity to venture very far from her home. So Edith was never exposed to the outside world. Edith attended a little high school in her rural county, and she ran track for her high school team. In fact, Edith was quite good. She was an amazing long-distance runner, and won every race in which she competed.

Edith led her team to the championship of their conference. As a reward, she and her team were invited to compete in the state championships in Birmingham.

Edith had never been to Birmingham. Or to any large city. So this trip was both exciting and intimidating at the same time. And to make things even more so, the state championships would be held at the same stadium where the University of Alabama Crimson Tide played its football games.

She had never seen anything quite so amazing as that stadium.

So when the time came for Edith's race, her senses were pretty overwhelmed.

Still, she was able to put all these distractions out of her mind and focus on the task at hand. In fact, she burned up the track that day!

She blasted right out of the starting blocks and grabbed the lead.

And as she came around the fourth turn, making her way toward the finish line, Edith was far, far ahead of the rest of the field.

Victory was assured.

First place was guaranteed.

The crowd was standing on their feet and roaring for her.

But suddenly, without warning, as she headed for the finish line Edith all at once pulled up short, and stopped dead in her tracks.

She stopped because she came face to face with an obstacle she had never encountered before.

An obstacle that in all of her great victories she'd never seen.

An obstruction she didn't know how to confront.

What was it?

It was a tape, stretched across the track at the finish line.

Edith had never seen a tape before! Not on a track!

She didn't know what to do. The crowd was screaming and roaring at her. Was she supposed to crawl under it? Was she supposed to jump over it? Had the race been halted? What was going on?

Never having seen a tape stretched across the finish line, Edith stood there and stared at it—

And stared at it—

She was transfixed—

Until the second-place runner finally caught up with her, and broke through the tape to take the blue ribbon.

So Edith lost the most important race of her life.

She was the fastest runner that day in the state of Alabama.

But just one foot short of the finish line, one stride short of victory, Edith quit running and failed to take her rightful place in racing history.

She failed to take her prize, because she failed to finish her course. She quit just inches shy of her goal, of her greatest achievement, because an unexpected obstacle caused her to stop running the race.

GETTING SIDETRACKED

I like this story, because it's indicative of the spiritual race many of us run.

We come so close!

We work so hard!

We endure for such a long, long time!

Then, for some reason, we give up, *right before we finish the race.*

Scripture is filled with examples of people like Edith, who quit when faced with some immovable obstacle.

Jesus said in the Parable of the Sower that we often allow "the cares of this world" or "the deceitfulness of riches" or "the lusts of other things" (Mark 4:19, KJV) to enter into the picture and deter us from our goal or distract us from our mission in life.

So there always seems to be *something* out there capable of distracting us or hindering us from finishing the course.

For Edith, it was a tape.

For me on the racetrack, it might be a flat tire.

A blown engine.

A part failure.

A bad call by an official.

Or maybe it's getting sidetracked by a crash somewhere on the track.

Trouble and hardships can sneak in, and distract you from finishing the race.

So you can't win any type of race until you learn to deal with these things.

You can't win at life either, until you learn to deal with the problems and hurdles of life that cause you to take your eyes off the finish line.

The victory.

Your triumph.

Your prize.

FIGHT TO THE FINISH

Whether you finish first, second, third, or in last place, God will reward you according to your effort and to how well you met or exceeded the expectations that were established for you in life.

So it's important for you to *compete.*

And it is important for you to *run well.*

It's important for you to *win.*

But the most important thing is never give up and to *finish the course.*

This truth was made very real to me through an experience I had at the Evergreen Speedway in Monroe.

It was a typical Saturday night at the track. The stands were packed with racing fans, and a lot of people showed up to watch The Rock Church Chevrolet in action and to cheer for our race team as we sped around the track.

But early in this particular 50-lap race, our driver got caught up in the middle of a big pileup coming out of turn 4.

The accident bent the car's front suspension and took the fenders off. The car wasn't totally destroyed though. It still ran. But it was really banged up, and in no condition to be competitive. So we pulled the car into the pit area.

Now typically in a situation like this, a driver will just park his car and wait for another day to race.

But we decided to try and repair the car, and finish the race. So my pit crew worked feverishly to get the car back in working order. And soon, after some major hustle and sweat by everybody on the team, I was pumping my fist in the air to see The Rock Church Chevrolet pulling back onto the track to challenge the other drivers.

Now let's be straight.

I knew there was no way we were going to win that day. Our car was about twenty laps behind the rest of the field, and that's an impossible deficit to make up in a 50-lap race.

But we weren't taking The Rock Church car back onto the track with the hope of winning.

We were getting back in the race with the intention of finishing, and placing as high as we could.

And finish we did.

And man, we would have liked to win.

After the race, a woman from our church approached me. I could tell she had something important to say. She was obviously impacted by something she'd witnessed during the race.

We started talking, and she told me about her teenage daughter, who was with her at the track that evening. It seems this girl was significantly affected by our decision to repair the car and take it back on the track. In recent weeks, she'd been struggling in a particular sport in high school. She was crushed and discouraged with her performance and wanted to quit.

This was the young lady's first experience with organized competition, and her parents were trying to encourage her to stick with it so she could grow and mature in her sport.

They were trying to teach her the life lesson of taking hold of a vision, and tenaciously pursuing it through thick and thin.

So when this teenage girl saw us take our Rock Church car back on the track that day, with absolutely zero possibility of winning the race, the power of that moment touched her.

She understood there was another way to claim victory.

To reject defeat.

It challenged her to rethink her own struggles with persistence.

It challenged her to believe she could overcome her obstacles.

And her mother wanted to thank us for not giving up.

FINISHING WHAT YOU STARTED

Challenges have a way of stopping us dead in our tracks sometimes.

But they can also be the spark that refuels us as we run our race.

The Apostle Paul used the analogy of racing to teach his young protégé Timothy the very same lesson.

Paul told him: "I have fought the good fight, I have finished the race, I have kept the faith. Now there is in store for me the crown of righteousness, which the Lord, the righteous Judge, will award to me on that day—and not only to me, but also to all who have longed for His appearing" (2 Timothy 4:7-8, NIV).

Now Paul didn't say he finished his race in first place.

He didn't say he took the gold medal.

Or the blue ribbon.

Or the checkered flag.

He didn't even say he placed high in the standings.

He simply told Timothy that he *finished his race.* And he told Timothy he was going to receive a prize, an everlasting crown of righteousness, simply because he chose to keep going until his race ended.

He didn't give up. And Paul promised the same eternal reward would be given to every man and woman who finished the race that God set before him or her.

It's about finishing what you started. Finishing is *winning.*

CHAPTER 10

A HEART OF TENACIOUS FAITH

This theme of tenacity continues as we dive into the book of Hebrews.

In Chapter 11, the writer defines faith as "the substance of things hoped for, the evidence of things not seen" (Hebrews 11:1, KJV).

The writer then shares a long list of great people who exhibited tenacious faith in their lives.

First off there's Noah, who by faith built the ark when there was no apparent reason to expect a flood.

Then there's Abraham, who by faith left his homeland and relocated to a strange new country simply because God told him to make the journey.

There's talk about Isaac, Jacob, Joseph, Moses, Samson, David, and others, *who through faith conquered kingdoms, administered justice, and gained what was promised; who shut the mouths of lions, quenched the fury of the flames, and escaped the edge of the sword; whose weakness was turned to strength; and who became powerful in battle and routed foreign armies.* (Hebrews 11:33-34, NIV).

Then, chapter 12 begins with the word *therefore*.

I like that word!

Therefore.

Whenever I see the word *therefore* in the Bible, I know God is getting ready to show me how the events of the previous verses can apply to my life in the here-and-now.

He's ready to bust out one of His most profound messages.

He's ready to show me how all those things that happened centuries ago can become His Game Plan for my life, and can impact my life in the 21st century.

<u>*Therefore*</u>, reads the book of Hebrews, *since we are surrounded by such a great cloud of witnesses, let us throw off everything that hinders and the sin that so easily entangles, and let us run with perseverance the race marked out for us* (Hebrews 12:1, NIV).

Now, if you think the Bible is boring and irrelevant, you've never really spent much time reading it. As a matter of fact, the Bible is anything but boring. It's totally thrilling!

Whip out your Bible, if you think I'm kidding, and flip through from Genesis to Exodus to Matthew to Revelation, and you'll see jaw-dropping true accounts of ordinary men and women doing extraordinary things.

All because of their tenacious faith in God!

And you'll read true accounts of the extraordinary things that an extraordinary God did through these ordinary people.

But these people were as different from one another as day is from night.

Some were rich and some were poor.

Some were highly educated and some were not educated at all.

Some were men.

Some were women.

But the common thread that connected them to one another was their shared faith in the Lord, and their amazing ability to trust Him in the most impossible situations.

Their lives had meaning beyond their corners of the globe and the times in which they lived.

Their lives still have meaning today, to you and me—because their lives serve as inspiration to us to run the same race of faith with perseverance.

And to make our own impact on the world by finishing the course God has given us to run.

This lesson of perseverance is a lesson I've learned, not just from the lives of these great men and women, but also from my own experiences on the racetrack, living my convictions and sharing my faith in a realm that can be difficult and challenging.

TAPPING INTO GOD WHEN THE TIDE TURNS

When I think of those who have inspired tenacious faith in me, two people rise to the top of the list.

My father.

And my mother.

And childhood memories of the bold faith my parents exhibited on a daily basis are still the stuff that rocks my world!

One of my favorite memories of my mother was seeing her at the start of each day sitting in her chair, reading the Bible and praying.

Mind you, at the same time as Mom was totally dialed-in to her Bible, I was scurrying about the house getting ready for school, putting on my jeans, brushing my teeth, combing my hair, chowing down on some Cap'n Crunch and generally wreaking havoc. But even with all the raging testosterone and the boyhood chatter I remember clogging up my brain, I can still flash back and hear Mom praying her bold morning prayers, totally tuned-in to God and without a single distraction.

She prayed for herself and for others.

I'm certain she prayed for you too. I know, sounds crazy. But she prayed a lot.

She also prayed for my sister, my dad, and me and asked God to bless the day for us and to use it to achieve His purposes in our lives.

I gotta tell you this memory has helped shape me into the person I am today, a memory that serves as an anchor in my life, fortifying my faith and reminding me of what's truly important.

And as I'd head out the door for school each day, Mom would always stop me and say the same thing:

"Son," she'd say, with a bold light in her eyes, "Everything you put your hand to today will prosper. And you'll have favor and high esteem from God and all those who look upon you."

These kinds of enduring memories have a way of changing you and reshaping you. They have a way of molding your character and your life.

I remember my father, too.

Dad was a steady and calm man. Especially after receiving Christ into his life, he demonstrated great wisdom, and he was the rock upon which our family stood in times of trouble. His voice soothing. It was reassuring and strong.

Through my father's voice, and my mother's prayers, I was inspired to run my own race with endurance.

From them I learned to refuse to give up when things got difficult. Bottom line?

Whether you're competing in a stock car race, in a high school sport, or in the race of life, you can count on two things.

First, it won't always be smooth sailing. At times, the battle will get intense and the tide may turn against you.

Second, as long as you stay in the race, you have a chance to win. If you quit, you're guaranteed failure.

But if you hang in there, you give yourself a chance to exceed expectations.

Hang in there and all things become possible.

Hang in there and you can tap into God's power in seemingly impossible situations.

SMALL STEPS LEAD TO BIG VICTORIES

In *The Revved Life*, small steps lead to big victories.

This is true in racing.

But it's even truer in life.

And it's true in doing our part to fulfill the Great Commission, too.

We can't get from the bottom to the top in one step, and God doesn't expect us to. Instead, the Lord expects us to do what Jonathan and his armor bearer did the day they led Israel to a mighty victory against the Philistines.

He expects us to climb the hill on the other side of the valley by using both hands and feet.

He expects us to scale the wall one inch at a time, until we finally reach the summit.

He expects us to grow "from glory to glory" (2 Corinthians 3:18, KJV), and to build our lives "here a little, and there a little" (Isaiah 28:10, KJV).

A perfect example of this in my life was the 2009 Fall Classic.

Normally, the races in which I compete are held on Saturday nights. But some really big races are held on Sunday afternoons. So once or twice a year, I'll take a Sunday off to compete in one of these prestigious races, where the purses are bigger and the publicity is greater.

The 2009 Fall Classic was like the Super Bowl and the World Series all rolled into one for my sport— the largest and most important stock car race in the Pacific Northwest. The Fall Classic came around just once a year, so this was one of those occasions when I wanted to do my best.

The race is always run at the Yakima Speedway in Central Washington. It consists of 200 laps, and my crew worked hard to get my car ready for this championship race. Instead of the usual 400-horsepower car, I would be racing my first "big-motor car," a monstrous 600-horsepower beast that accelerated faster than the smaller powered cars I was accustomed to driving.

This would be my first race in a car with that much horsepower, so I spent a lot of time practicing the day before the race. In fact, I practiced continuously for the two days *prior* to the race. But I still felt unsure of myself behind the wheel and nervous about the car. I simply didn't have the experience with the power to drive with confidence.

My uncertainty became obvious as I qualified in 28th position for the race. In a field of 42 cars, this would put me right in the middle of the pack and far from the front.

My dilemma was: I *really* wanted to drive my smaller car! My reliable Chevrolet didn't have quite as much power or acceleration as this big-motor car, but I felt completely at ease with it. I was comfortable. I was sure I could run up front with *that car*.

Nevertheless, I decided not to revert to my old, familiar chariot. The team worked hard, had busted their butts on this high horsepower car, and they'd put everything into getting it ready for the race. I just couldn't bring myself to disappoint them at the last minute.

So I did what my mom and dad had taught me.

I decided to push through.

Now I'm positive the guys could tell something was bothering me. But I never let on that it was the car. I hoped they figured that I was just extra nervous before the big race. Who am I kiddin,' they could see my struggle at dinner Saturday night.

As the sun rose that Sunday morning, I decided to stick with my normal routine just as if I was preparing to preach at The Rock Church. Only today instead of jeans, button up shirt, and some nice shoes I'd get to wear three layers of Nomex (fire retardant material), driving shoes and a Bell Helmet.

My morning began.

I ate a bowl of Cap'n Crunch.

I spent a little time reading the Bible.

I prayed for a while.

And then I left the motor home to fulfill my God-given purpose for that day.

I'm glad I decided to stick with my normal routine, because God used it to do something truly amazing and life changing for me.

LUCKY DOGS AND ATTITUDE ADJUSTMENTS

It happened as I was thumbing through my Bible in preparation for the race.

As I was flipping through the book of Samuel, I came across the little story of Jonathan, the son of King Saul and David's best friend.

In this story, Jonathan and his armor bearer decided to do something about a standoff that had been dragging on between the army of Israel and the Philistine army. For a while now, these two armies had faced off, watching each other from a distance, and mocking each other from opposite sides of the valley.

But Jonathan was fed up. He was tired of the games.

He was tired of the inactivity and the indecision that bred nothing but fear in the hearts of his comrades.

So Jonathan defied the orders of his father, King Saul, and decided to cross the valley alone and climb the hill on the opposite side so he could start killing Philistines.

He believed that his fellow soldiers would follow his example if he just did something bold. And he believed God would give Israel a great victory because of his brave actions.

So Jonathan turned to his armor bearer and said, "Come on, climb right behind me, for the Lord will help us defeat them" (1 Samuel 14:12, NLT).

That little verse impacted me in a powerful way.

With that powerful verse buzzing in my brain, God really put the hammer down and hit me.

As I was preparing to leave for the racetrack, the Lord spoke to me and said, "Jeff, small steps lead to big victories."

That message stopped me in my tracks. Now, when you hear a message like that, let's face it, you'd better listen with both your ears and your whole heart, because the Almighty is bringing you a God-sized vision.

I realized that this verse would be significant for me that day, and I wrote it on a piece of tape, which I placed on the dashboard of my car directly in front of me, where I could see it during the race.

And I'm sure glad I did! Because that verse and the thought God planted in my heart that morning gave me a brand new perspective on things.

It gave me an attitude adjustment about the car and the race.

And when the race started, I totally zeroed-in on putting the #70 car in the winner's circle, and I just raced my heart out.

I put my head down and concentrated on what I was supposed to do, focusing on each corner and giving that lap my very best as I thundered around the track.

I focused on the *small steps* that go into racing.

Be smooth.

Hit my marks.

Pay attention to the weight transfer.

Roll the center.

And a thousand other racecar jargons.

But the race was marred with an excessive number of crashes.

And that produced a large number of caution flags.

Because this was the last race of the year and the biggest, nobody was interested in racing conservatively. Every driver was intent on pulling out all the stops and driving full throttle.

So by the time we came to lap 165, a lot of cars crashed and a lot of time passed, three-and-a-half hours to be exact, and I found myself completely stopped once again on the track, sitting there in my car under a red flag.

And while I was sitting there, I used my two-way radio to communicate with my spotter, Steve.

"What position am I in?" I asked.

"You're in sixth place, the first car one lap down," Steve said. "If you get another caution, you'll have the *lucky dog* and be on the lead lap." The *lucky dog* is a rule that allows the first car one lap down to gain back a lap and restart at the tail end of the lead lap.

My face broke into a huge grin, hearing I might get that lucky dog and a free pass back to the lead lap.

And as I sat there stopped on the track I thought to myself:

Wow! Sixth place! I can't believe it! This was the biggest race of the year. All the best drivers were competing, and all of them were giving it everything they had.

And when I considered the fact I started in 28th place, I was amazed to be so close to the lead. Plus, I was just one caution flag away from getting back onto the lead lap. So if I could keep doing what I was doing, I might be able to work my way to the top of the pack and actually challenge the guys up front for the podium.

Let me tell you, I had a huge head full of steam by the time the race restarted. I continued doing what I'd been doing for the past three-and-a-half hours. I put my head down, and focused on the car in front of me.

I threw caution to the wind, and rolled up to the lead cars.

Sure enough, after another caution and restart I was back on the lead lap, competing for fifth place. I was pumped!

With eight laps remaining in the race I had settled into 5th, with my sites on 4th.

All of a sudden, out of nowhere a driver who was 37 laps down lost control, and took me out. I slid the length of the backstretch trying to save my trusty steed.

Wham! I hit a gigantic tire in the infield, placed there to protect the stadium lighting for the racing surface. It sheered the nose of my car right off.

I was, shall we say with a loving pastoral voice, "P!$$ed OFF!"

Even though we made it roll, and finished under power my day ended by my #70 car coming to the pits for repairs, losing a lap, and finishing eighth in the race.

Still, that was a life-changing experience for me. Not only had this been the biggest race of my life, but the 2009 Fall Classic became a turning point for me attitudinally.

In racing and in life, small steps do lead to big victories. No one gets to the top in a day, it's a culmination of constant and continued persistence which brings the victory.

That day I didn't win the car race. I did win another nugget for life.

In fact, I still have that piece of tape from my dashboard displayed in my toolbox to remind me of the spiritual lesson I learned that day.

CHAPTER 11

A HEART THAT SHOWS UP EVERY SINGLE DAY

God's work has its own pace.

God works in *His* time.

God doesn't pull off a miracle, and then disappear from your life in a cloud of dust.

God shows up, Every. Single. Day.

No matter what.

And every single day, God expects us to grow in faith and wisdom.

He also expects us to become better mothers.

Fathers.

Men.

Women.

Sons.

Daughters.

Disciples.

But He doesn't expect to see it in one giant leap.

Jesus sees our growth incrementally, one step at a time. Jesus is committed to us for the long haul.

And just as Jesus created physical things—plants, trees, animals, children—to grow slowly and steadily, so He designed the believer to grow slowly and steadily.

A person living *The Revved Life* is not a man or woman who has seemingly achieved perfection in life, or who goes from the valley to the mountaintop in one giant leap.

When you live *The Revved Life*, you learn.

Grow.

Improve.

And change.

Every single day.

Living *The Revved Life* means you tackle life head-on and learn from day-to-day how to approach, touch, impact, and help other people meet the Lord.

Someone living *The Revved Life* is an ordinary *Joe* like you and me— but they're a person who's spent time with Jesus, has been impacted and changed by the Lord, and who's learning day by day to walk the walk of faith.

And to talk the talk of faith.

In the parts that follow, I want to show you how ordinary people who've spent time with Christ can truly impact the lives of those around them.

But as I prepare to share those insights with you, I want you to start by grasping this core concept of *The Revved Life:*

That all great journeys begin with small steps.

A little step here and a little step there can add up to a whole lifetime of forward progress.

Progress that can take you farther than you ever thought you'd go.

And here's the cool thing and the most beautiful part of it:

I learned this from racing!

Not only has the racetrack become my second pulpit of ministry for the Lord; it's also the place where I find personal fulfillment.

Scripture says the Apostle Paul saw the racetrack as a place of spiritual enlightenment, as well. By watching chariot racers and runners compete in the games of his day, Paul discovered the great spiritual lessons that would shape his life, and drive his destiny.

And he discovered a forceful analogy for the Christian life.

Through the analogy of racing, I've also discovered many life-changing truths.

So let's embrace these truths and give God the high-fives for them.

Let's also impart these truths to others.

Most importantly, let's *live* them.

Let's put them into practice in our own lives.

And let's become winners—sharing our passion for Christ—not just on the racetrack, but in life.

And let's prepare to win others to the Lord, also.

Because that's our chief occupation and our primary purpose in this world.

Living *The Revved Life.*

PART 3

THE PROFILE OF *THE REVVED LIFE*

CHAPTER 12

THE MESSENGER

When they saw the courage of Peter and John and realized that they were unschooled, ordinary men, they were astonished and they took note that these men had been with Jesus.

—Acts 4:13, NIV

*T*he Revved Life is a mission.

Those living it have a message to share with the world.

Something important to say.

Now you might be thinking: "I'm a Christ-follower, Jeff! I've got something important to share!"

But before you can become a poster child for living *The Revved Life,* and before you can really speak into another person's life, you have to show that you actually have something *worth saying.*

Something *worth hearing.*

You must start *becoming who you've been created to be*—and *live The Revved Life*—before you can jump in with your big boy pants on, and complete the mission.

I started this book by sharing the insights I'd gained on the racetrack and in my life, regarding the behaviors of a bold believer. Now I want to share my insights about the methods someone living *The Revved Life* can use to win *others* to Christ.

Before I do that, let's press the "pause" button on that conversation a minute, so I can remind you how essential it is to *live* a winning life, before you can effectively *share* a winning message.

Why?

Because the Bible and nature teach us that actions speak louder than words—and that people want to *see* and *be convinced* of the integrity of the messenger, before they will believe his message.

In a lot of areas of life, it's possible to separate the message from the messenger.

A math teacher, for instance, can be the worst-dressed slob in the teacher's lounge, with horrible breath and a mullet even a trucker wouldn't rock, and still teach math well.

A basketball coach can be a complete chain-smoking social misfit, who yells and screams at his players and looks like he's been bingeing on candy and caffeine all weekend, and still motivate them to compete at a high level.

But when it comes to sharing the amazing Word of God, God's messenger cannot get away with this kind of duplicity!

In the work of God, the message and the messenger *are one.*

They are *the same!*

People will judge the message by the messenger. And they will judge the messenger by his message.

So it's vital to *become who Jesus created you to be*, before you can attempt to *do what Jesus created you to do.*

Don't get that confused. Before *you do* anything amazing, *you are* already amazing! Before you deliver at a high level you are already delivered at a high level.

There's no getting around it. It's absolutely vital to run your own race of life with excellence, with passion, and with boldness, and to run it to win.

Run it fearlessly.

Run it with dignity.

Run it with tenacity.

And run it with purpose and endurance, as you take those small steps every single day to finish the course God has set before you.

Then, and only then, will you have the platform from which to speak with authority and conviction into the lives of those watching you.

Then, and only then, will you have credibility—the kind that commands the respect and attention of those to whom you speak.

Then, and only then, will your words have the power to leave their mark, and to change hearts and minds.

BE RIGHT ON THE INSIDE, NOT ON THE OUTSIDE

Let's be clear though.

Your authority to speak effectively for Christ does not come from your status in the community.

Or your achievements in the work place.

Or your title.

Your educational accomplishments.

Or your sports trophies.

Or your net worth.

"Say what, Jeff?," you're probably saying to yourself right now.

It's the hard truth.

Your authority to speak for our Lord comes solely from your relationship with Him. It is from this position and relationship with Jesus, and the impact He has made on your performance, that you achieve this thing called life.

It's nothing you've done.

Or earned.

Or deserve.

It's all because of Jesus!

You have to *know* Jesus, before you can become his Go-To-Guy for spreading His Word.

You have to have seen that God will show up, in a big way, to speak with boldness about being His humble servant.

You might be thinking, "Well, Jeff, maybe I'm not ready to be a witness for Jesus. I don't have time to speak boldly right now. I'm just an ordinary Joe Blow, with a boring job, no benefits, a mountain of bills, a beat-up car, yada yada yada …"

Not all of us have the same occupations. But all of us have the same human challenges.

Not all of us have the same interests. But all of us have the same doubts and fears.

Not all of us have the same resources. But we all have the same brief amount of time to live our lives, and then to slip into eternity, where we will come face to face with God.

This is why Jesus chose *ordinary* men to follow Him! This is why He chose *ordinary* men and *ordinary* women to represent Him! This is why He chose *ordinary* people to serve Him!

To worship Him.

And to speak on His behalf to a world in desperate need of knowing Him.

And this is what caught the attention of the Jewish elders of that day. To speak of Peter and John as *ordinary* men was not disrespectful.

As a matter of fact, it was quite a compliment.

Peter and John—and the rest of the believers—did not gain their wisdom and boldness through the acquisition of fancy titles. Their ability to grasp the Scriptures and passionately defend their faith wasn't gained through formal education. They didn't learn to speak with clarity and power by attending a weekend self-help seminar.

These men were changed because *they'd been with Jesus.*

And they were fearless because they were eyewitnesses to the resurrection.

Can you imagine?

They saw the miracles of God's mighty power every single day.

Crippled beggars stood up and walked, at the sound of their voices!

Sinners repented, and surrendered their lives to Jesus, at their words!

Men, women and children were miraculously healed—simply because *the shadow of Peter fell upon them!*

In the days that followed, the members of the Sanhedrin (the Jewish council of elders) were shocked to realize that these ordinary men had the power to withstand persecution.

To stand tall to the Sanhedrin's threats!

To walk out of securely locked prison cells!

And to cause liars and deceivers to fall dead at their feet!

Now something was obviously and undeniably different about Peter, John, and all the rest of these *ordinary men* who had spent time with Christ.

And that's the message I'm trying to convey here.

If you want to be a soul winner for Christ, you must first become a winning soul.

If you want to change the lives of others, you must *first* be changed yourself.

In the world, you can be dishonest and greedy and still succeed in business. You can lie and be lustful and still succeed as a leader. You can be selfish and crude and still find a cure for cancer.

You can even be a vile and despicable human being and still win a sports championship.

But in the kingdom of God, it doesn't work that way.

In God's world, you can't separate a man's character from a man's message.

You can't separate his relationship with Christ from his destiny in life.

I can't stress strongly enough how important it is for the man and woman of God to get his life right with the Lord, before he gets his message right for his audience.

From God's view, it's more important to be right on the *inside* than to seem right on the *outside*.

And the only way to see genuine and enduring results from your words is to make sure that those words have substance in your own life, before you share them with others.

ORDINARY PEOPLE

Think about this:

Peter and John, like all effective believers, were not renowned for what they knew.

Or where they had been.

Or what they had achieved.

No way!

They were renowned for *who* they knew.

They were just *ordinary* guys, but they had been with Jesus.

And because they had been with Jesus, they were changed men, their futures had been transformed, and their lives showed it.

They had seen a lot of incredible stuff, and they had heard a lot. And because the things they had seen and heard made such a tremendous impact on them, others were willing to listen to them when they shared their insights and wisdom.

And others were willing to believe them, when they spoke about their personal experiences.

But if Peter and John and the rest of the believers were really just ordinary Joe's and Jake's, like you and me, what was it that set them apart?

What gave their words credibility?

What made it obvious to others that these absolutely ordinary men had been with the Messiah, the Savior, the King of Kings, with Jesus?

What was it that caused even demonic spirits to step back and flee these unconventional men?

THEY WERE UNCONVENTIONAL IN THE WAY THEY WITNESSED

Think about this:

An effective witness for God will always have an unconventional manner for presenting the Gospel.

Always!

Now, what I'm going to say next flies all up in the face of this. And that is:

Sometimes, in the body of Christ, there is a subtle insistence upon conformity.

Many of us Christians seem more willing to accept others, as long as those "other people" believe everything we believe.

If they do all the same things we do.

If they dress like us.

If they drive the same car as we do.

If they shop at the same Wal-Mart.

If they blast the same music on their iPod.

If they watch the same movies.

And share the same friends.

And newcomers seem to pick up real quick on this tendency to conform—maybe it's our instinct to survive, or the praise that gets heaped on them for getting on good ground with the whole "God thing"— because they usually get in line with other Christians, right away.

In some ways, this flipping-on-the-conformity switch can be a pretty awesome thing.

No, seriously! People tend to follow great leadership. Let's stop for a moment to consider a couple of things:

Number One: I have noticed that new converts sometimes seek to emulate many of the choices and behaviors of the more mature Christians in the congregation.

If someone new to faith thinks you're a good example, and they're hungry to learn why, that new person will buy the same Bible that you have and will read the same books that you read. They will sit in the same row at church and watch when you raise your hand in worship. In fact, most new believers get so psyched and pumped-up and excited about their new life in Christ and to have the name Jesus tattooed on their heart that they just want to become your best buddy, and be just like you in every way.

Why? They want to get as far away from their old lives and their old friends as possible!

They want to change their behavior completely!

So they are looking for someone to tell them how to toss their old behavior in the dumpster and teach them what their new life should look like.

You become their model.

You become one of the building blocks in the new life they're constructing.

So this natural inclination for new Christians to latch on and follow in the footsteps of established Christians is not an unusual or a bad thing. In fact, it's a necessary ingredient in the discipleship process.

Just as a young child emulates his parents, so a new believer will emulate his pastor and other Christians he admires in their attitudes, speech, and behaviors.

And in the same way a child eventually grows up and starts developing his own attitudes and his own ability to think for himself, the believer eventually comes to the place where he learns to make choices on his own, based on the guidance of God's Word in his own heart, not upon the demands of other Christians.

Or the Christian community at large.

Or anyone else.

Just Jesus.

CHAPTER 13

THE LAW OF DIFFERENCE

The Number Two thing I want you to consider is this:

Throughout the Bible, there is an undeniable *law of difference* that finds its expression in the life of the child of God.

Simply stated, this spiritual *law* compels us to realize that God makes people *different*.

And that a person's spiritual gifts are usually discovered when he recognizes *that thing* which sets him apart from other people.

In his first letter to the Corinthians, the Apostle Paul explains that God gives different spiritual gifts to different believers (see 1 Corinthians 12:4-6).

You probably see it all the time. While one believer might excel in public speaking, another one excels in music.

And while one does amazing work for the Lord on the stage under the spotlight, another stands out best behind the scenes and out of sight.

You see, God gives people different spiritual capacities in the same way He gives people different physical and mental capacities.

Just think about it!

God made our bodies.

He made our souls.

He created our spirits.

We have no problem understanding the *law of difference* on that level. When it comes to the physical body, we all recognize that people have different physical capacities. A 6'4" NFL linebacker can lift the back end of V-8 half-ton pickup truck off the ground. But a small, elderly woman may have trouble lifting her own body out of a chair.

Likewise, we have no problem understanding the *law of difference* on the mental, emotional, or social levels (the level of the soul). I mean, anyone who's attended school knows that some students pick up math quicker and remember historical dates more easily than other students. And while some 12-year-old girls have the maturity of a young adult, some college-aged guys can do the most surprisingly immature things.

So okay: we understand the biblical *law of difference* on the physical level and on the mental, emotional, and social levels. But while we grasp this concept on these *natural* levels, we have the hardest time understanding it on the *spiritual* level.

Nevertheless, the same kind of *difference* that exists in the natural realm also exists in the spiritual realm.

On the natural level, we quickly notice and accept the differences that exist between people. No one person has all the skills needed in life—but every person has at least one skill.

And every person's skill—whether it's writing songs, building websites, calculating taxes, or overhauling engines—sets him apart from his peers, and that makes him valuable to the community.

But when it comes to the spiritual dimension of life, we have a hard time grasping this concept!

We somehow have convinced ourselves that every person—every Christian—should be the same.

But the facts tell quite a different story.

And the Bible tells quite a different story.

YOUR MEASURE OF FAITH

One thing the Bible makes clear is that God gives every man a "measure of faith."

—Romans 12:3, NIV

So your faith is not the same as my faith.

And my faith is not the same as my wife's faith.

The Bible also makes it clear that God gives spiritual gifts according to His pleasure (see 1 Corinthians 12:7-11). So the spiritual abilities God's given me won't be the same as the spiritual abilities He's given to you. That's why my race of life won't be compared to yours on Judgment Day. I will be judged, based on what I've done with the unique gifts God has placed at my disposal.

That's also why as a Christian I need you and why you need me.

It's why the various members of the church have to learn to get along and to draw from one another's strengths while they help each other overcome their weaknesses.

What you have, I don't have.

And what I have, you don't have.

So there is *something* that makes me different from you, and there is *something* that makes you different from me.

And my job is to discover, embrace, and develop the unique talents and qualities that God has given to me so that I can fulfill God's unique calling on my life.

Which is different from His unique calling on your life.

Your life and your journey for God is none of my business—except for my responsibility to pray for you and to encourage you along the way.

And my life and journey are none of your business.

Maybe your uniqueness will be found in your appearance.

Maybe it will be found in your mental abilities.

Or your personality.

I don't know what *your difference* is. The only thing I know for certain is that God made you different from everyone else.

And while some of your buddies at work or in the neighborhood might learn to despise the thing that makes them different, it's precisely that difference that God wants to use in your life.

Why? So you can do something meaningful for Him.

THE THING THAT MAKES YOU DIFFERENT

What made Samson *different?*

Do you think it was his strength?

His long hair?

I bet all the other kids made fun of Samson when he was young. And I bet his brothers and sisters teased him until he cried. But those are exactly the things that God used to unleash Samson's power and impact the world through Samson's life.

What made Esther *different?* Do you suppose it was her beauty? I bet that put Esther in a ton of compromising situations when she was growing up, and I'm sure that a lot of boys bugged her for dates and a lot of girls hated her as a teenager. But while many young women might try to hide their beauty in order to be accepted by the other girls or to avoid harassment by hot-to-trot guys, Esther learned to embrace her God-given gift. Esther's beauty propelled her to the throne. It enabled her to save the Jewish people from annihilation while they were exiled in Persia.

What made David *different?* David played with his slingshot the same way young boys today play video games. And David played his harp with the same passion that young men nowadays shred a guitar solo in their local band. But God used the harp to usher David into the courts of King Saul, and He used the slingshot to catapult David to greatness when he killed Goliath. So both of these special skills became instrumental in elevating David from obscurity to the throne of Israel.

So here's the deal: don't despise *that thing* which makes you different.

And don't be afraid to be different.

It's the unexpected.

The unconventional.

It's the unusual that command the fascination of the masses.

And it's the unconventional and the unexpected that God uses to crash open the doors of opportunity, in order to establish His people in places where they can serve Him and represent Him to an entire culture of lost souls.

Show me two people who are exactly alike …

And I'll show you one who's unnecessary.

You are a unique creation! And God designed you that way for a reason.

You have your own unique fingerprint.

Your own unique DNA coding.

Your own unique retinal scan.

And you have your own unique destiny and purpose.

God made you *different* to fulfill your special purpose in the church and in the world, the two places He wants you to serve Him most.

So keep in mind that God created each of us to be a one-shot. A one-of-a-kind.

So don't be afraid to be *different*.

UNCONVENTIONAL, UNCOMMON, AND UNORTHODOX

The truly great Christians have been men and women with unconventional approaches to life and ministry.

I just told you about David. David took his slingshot into battle against Goliath, because David felt strong and comfortable rockin' his slingshot. His ability with this weapon was one of those unconventional abilities that God gave to him for his watershed moment in history.

That's why David refused to take King Saul's armor into battle against Goliath. You see, David wasn't comfortable with someone else's weaponry. He wasn't familiar with someone else's style.

Saul's armor didn't "fit" David. It didn't fit his body, and it didn't fit his method of doing battle.

David won his battle with Goliath by embracing the unusual and unique talent that God gave him.

But here's the weird thing: I look around and I see Christians breaking their necks all over the place in an effort to copy and emulate other believers who are doing great things for the Lord.

These copycats want to preach like T.D. Jakes.

They want to sing like Joel Houston and Hillsong United.

They want to build a church like Joel Osteen.

They want to write books like Rick Warren.

But here's the deal: God doesn't want you to be like anybody except Jesus! He wants you to be *you*.

He wants you to be unique!

Distinctive!

Unconventional!

He wants you to be original!

Uncommon!

Unorthodox!

He wants you to find the way to represent Him that works best for you—and that demands the respect and recognition of those who know the *real you*.

I found my unique way of serving the Lord at the racetrack.

And I've taken a lot of heat and a ton of grief for it, especially from Christians who don't understand the *law of difference*.

But just like the Apostle Paul, I know who I am in Christ.

I know my purpose.

I know my destiny. I know my God-given assignment.

And most of all, I know that nobody else can take my place.

Seriously, if I back down from my destiny in order to satisfy those who don't understand the uniqueness that God's placed within me, I will be abandoning my assignment in life.

I'll be betraying God's purpose for me.

And I'll be leaving an entire subculture of lost souls to the enemy. I also will live my life unfulfilled.

I'd be a flop and an epic failure for the Lord.

Because I wouldn't be who God made me to be.

Once again, I learned this valuable life lesson from my parents.

See, my mom and dad weren't afraid to be themselves or to approach life and ministry in unconventional ways. My mom, particularly, was exceptional in her one-of-a-kind representation of the King of Kings and the Lord of Lords.

My mom didn't push Jesus to the backseat. She knew who was at the wheel, driving her destiny.

My mom didn't need a GPS, to know God was always pointing her life in the right direction.

REACH THE UNREACHED

Now I've already told you about the little Bible study my parents started in their house, shortly after they were saved.

You already heard how their small home Bible study grew into a great church.

But what you don't know yet is how they went about building that Bible study, and reaching the unreached.

Engaging the unengaged.

Seeking the lost.

When they were first saved, my parents didn't know Jack about the Bible. So they were entirely incapable of teaching the Bible to others.

At their little study group, they would play these sermon cassette tapes, and the people would sit around our living room and listen.

But my parents were smart enough to realize that God's children needed some amped-up music too.

After all, nothing is worse than a Christian gathering without awesome music and an atmosphere of worship.

The trouble was, nobody was available to play an instrument except this one lone dude who knew how to play the same three chords on an acoustic guitar.

Oh, and he only knew a single song.

So my mom did something pretty crazy and unconventional.

One day, she went down to a place called Petosa's, the local restaurant and hang-out bar, and started talking to members of the band who were playing there. Locally, there were events called "battle of the bands," and Mom listened to all of them. She picked her favorite one and started praying for their salvation.

And she somehow convinced 4 out of 6 of them to come to her Bible study. They'd bring their amps and instruments, turn up the volume and away we'd go. The music these guys played was far from conventional Christian stuff; they didn't know any Christian songs—not even *Amazing Grace*!

And even though everything they played sounded like *Sweet Home Alabama,* it was real, and in a few short weeks the whole team learned to use music in worship! Somehow, my mom managed to build our church's first music department by getting people far from God to come play for God in her home.

And she and my dad built a great church by opening their house to anybody who would come.

And eventually, those band members that my mom recruited from the local bar went on to accept Jesus Christ as their Savior! In fact, they became pastors and staff members over the next several years.

Awesome!

These guys were set free from addictions, and became incredible Christ-followers, rising up other musicians for this growing congregation.

So apparently, my mom and dad were doing something right!

CHAPTER 14

A PATH OUTSIDE THE LINES

A sk yourself this question: Why was Jesus crucified?

Jesus was crucified because of His unorthodox approach to ministry!

And His experience before and after he was nailed to the cross teaches us a lesson:

That religious people will both reject you and persecute you, if you decide to take a path in life that falls anywhere outside the lines.

But while the church does have a tendency to create clones out of newbies and baby Christians, the world outside the church is searching for something different.

Something unique.

Something genuine.

They are just waiting for all of us Christians to leave the confines of our comfy church buildings and our velvet-lined pews, and to engage them in the "real world."

They are waiting for God-loving men and women to interact with them in the reality of their lives.

It was by the grace of God that I learned this *law of difference* one day, many years ago.

And because it hit me like a pro football lineman going after the quarterback, and God in that awesome moment shared His truth with me, several NASCAR™ drivers now attend my church, and plan to spend eternity with me up in heaven.

Touchdown!

In fact, the full-tilt impact of our church's outreach to the racing community was driven home to me, back in the Fall of 2011.

It was Pastor Appreciation Month at The Rock Church, and our leadership team came together to plan a special event to say "thank you" to Melinda and me for our many years of service.

Now at that event, the leaders of the church asked all those who had been saved, through the church's racing ministry, to join Melinda and me on the platform.

You want to talk about a great stage? Man, the stage that day was jam-packed and overflowing with saved drivers, pit crewmembers and a ton of race fans! And this gave me and everyone else in attendance a powerful vision—a confirmation—of God's favor on our work.

It also inspired us to do more to break down the walls and the confines of tradition, and to reach beyond the doors of our church to touch those who needed Christ.

So every Sunday morning, the seats at The Rock Church are now packed with guys and their wives and their families who have come to Christ simply because I chose to drive a racecar, and to get involved in a world that was new and uncharted to me.

Over the years, many of these converts have become leaders in the effort to win souls and disciple others.

They work alongside me every week, to proclaim the good news of Christ to those who don't know Him, and to help me build a strong and enduring church for those who do.

And these precious co-workers are there by my side because I refused to listen to the worn-out, frightened, ineffective message of caution and timidity that emanates from many Christians.

I chose to listen to the boldness of our Lord instead, and to that amazing and life-transforming thing He was whispering into my ear, regarding my place in His kingdom, and my unique role in His service.

I chose my path.

I chose my destiny.

I chose to be unconventional.

THEY WERE BOLD BEYOND THEIR LIMITATIONS

I want you to think back with me for a second.

Think back, to the day and the moment you first got saved.

In the beginning, when you were saved, your new Christian life was unbelievably exciting.

There's seriously nothing like it.

If you've made that commitment, you can probably remember what it was like.

You wanted to go to church all the time.

You wanted to worship all day, every day.

You wanted to be around your Christian friends morning, noon, and night.

You wanted to give and serve and sing loud and read your Bible every chance you got.

Over time, however, all Christians realize that there is another element to the Christian life—the element of opposition and persecution. Some people will enjoy hearing about your newfound faith!

But others won't.

And you learn this lesson quickly.

Those people who fail to appreciate your joy in being saved by Jesus Christ will challenge you.

And mock you.

They'll scorn you.

And even persecute you.

The early believers went through this same process. They saw this unleashing of persecution on their heads. On the Day of Pentecost, when the Holy Spirit came on the early Christians in an awe-inspiring, dramatic manner, those members of the Jerusalem church were pumped-up with excitement and enormous enthusiasm.

As a result, they devoted themselves to the apostles' teaching (see Acts 2:42).

They also devoted themselves to the growing fellowship—to the sharing of meals with other believers, and to prayer.

I mean, these guys were totally locked-in to the Gospel. They even sold their possessions, so they could help meet the financial needs of the other members of the church (see Acts 2:45).

And because of all these amazing things, the church grew rapidly in numbers and in favor (see Acts 2:47; 5:13-14).

But this is where their world became a battleground.

And this is where the war to save souls began.

God wants us to leave the familiar, comfortable environment of our Christian friends and our bonds of fellowship, and to engage in the unbelieving world with the doubters, and the naysayers.

He wants us to come locked-and-loaded with the Gospel.

He wants us to do battle with the enemy.

He wants us to confront disbelief.

Wrestle evil.

Fight sin.

And stand up, get in a cage and fight with spiritual rebellion.

But what does this mean?

This means that we are going to have to be ready for conflict.

We have to be ready for opposition.

We have to be prepared to sign up for battle.

THE MESSAGE OF THIS BOOK IN A NUTSHELL

The apostles were ready for this battle. Even though they enjoyed their wonderful season of growth and popularity, they knew their purpose in life was much bigger than this temporary victory.

They knew their mission was much greater.

They knew their mission was to approach people with the Word of God, and confront them with their need for Jesus Christ.

So that's exactly what they did.

And immediately—BOOM!—they met the full force of opposition that the Lord promised to those who would dare to boldly represent Him to an unreceptive world.

First up, Peter and John were arrested for healing a crippled beggar, and for telling people that the beggar had been healed through the magnificent power of Jesus Christ.

And because of this proclamation, the persecution began.

Peter and John were tossed into prison, to intimidate and to create fear in their hearts.

The members of the Sanhedrin wanted the apostles to know that they were at the mercy of this powerful body of leaders. But Peter and John weren't intimidated. They weren't frightened. They weren't demoralized, or deterred from their mission.

Instead, the apostles were encouraged.

And emboldened.

Matter of fact, when asked to give an accounting for the healing they performed, Peter boldly refused to soften his message as he stood before the council. Being as politically incorrect as he possibly could be, he courageously told the Sanhedrin that they had just crucified the Son of God, and that the "stone you builders rejected" had become the capstone in God's plan for saving humanity (see Acts 3:10-12).

Now the Bible tells us that the Sanhedrin were impressed. They weren't *changed*, but they were *impressed*. And what were they impressed by?

Three things:

They were impressed by Peter's courage.

They were impressed by the indisputable fact that these men had been with Jesus.

And they were impressed that these guys were obviously just *ordinary men*.

Wow! That pretty much says it all, right? I could just about stop here and send this manuscript to press right now.

In fact, that's the whole message of this book in a nutshell.

You might think you're just an ordinary guy, with boring friends and a boring life and a boring job.

But you too, have a destiny in the Lord.

And there is an element of your destiny that is unique to you, and that separates you from everyone else.

You don't have to be rich.

Or smart.

Or beautiful.

Or prestigious.

You don't have to be famous, powerful, or influential.

Because God uses uneducated, *ordinary people* to do His work.

God uses people who have *been with Jesus* to touch and change the world.

But most importantly, God uses *courageous* people to do His work.

So you don't have to hang your head, thinking you're too ordinary to be used by God.

But you do have to be *bold*.

And boldness is the result of spending time with the Lord.

BE BOLD

The boldness of Peter and John is what captured the attention of the elders.

Their boldness and the way they could rise up against persecution, oppression, torture, and threats touched and changed everybody who saw and heard it, and opened the doors of opportunity for the apostles to share their faith.

Believe it or not, the Sanhedrin decided to release Peter and John *because* of their boldness! They saw these guys ready to pay a tremendous price for their faith in Jesus, and stopped short of punishing them.

They simply let them go.

What's the message here?

Don't be afraid to be unconventional in your efforts to reach people for Christ.

No offense to any of you old-school Christians: but it's obvious the traditional methods of evangelism haven't been all that effective.

So maybe a new approach might be smart.

And while we're being unconventional, let's be sure to ask God to help us be bold.

If you have a bold attitude, you can use it to your advantage as you approach people with the Gospel. But if you lack boldness, you can still pray the same prayer that the early church prayed after Peter and John were released from prison.

Ask God to make you bold. Then get out there in your own unique way and rock your faith.

Now I hear some of you shooting back that being bold is not that simple. I'll give you some practical pointers later on.

And don't be afraid of the flak. Be confident! Take charge of yourself and your environment.

You may be *ordinary* in every other respect. But if you are representing Christ in the place where God has set you—

And if you are operating in harmony with your own talents and gifts—

And if you have *been with Jesus* and committed your life to Him—

Then strap on your seatbelt and get ready for an electrifying, high-octane, wind-in-your-face ride—because you can be confident that the Lord will step up and use you in an awesome way.

Boldness flows from the confidence that you are doing the right thing.

And doing it in the right way.

And doing it at the right time.

And doing it in the right place.

Be bold.

RISK TAKING FAITH

It would be pretty arrogant of me to put myself on the same level as Peter and John. So don't misunderstand what I'm trying to say.

But I can't help but notice and be awed by so many similarities between their experiences in Jerusalem, and my experiences at the racetrack.

Check this out: Peter and John were just minding their own business, going to the temple to pray one day. They had no intentions of stirring up conflict, or causing trouble for themselves. But when they healed the crippled beggar, and when they started telling the curious spectators about Jesus and his miraculous resurrection, they found themselves pretty pronto in direct opposition to the ruling elders.

They found themselves on trial.

They found themselves facing punishment.

This episode in the lives of Peter and John reminds me of the day I made the decision to combine racing with ministry.

You see, I wasn't looking to provoke anyone that day. I was simply going to the track to see my new car and to watch my team join the chase for the checkered flag for the very first time.

I was just minding my own business, but I quickly found myself in a situation where I had to either speak up for the Lord or zip my lip and stay silent.

I had to either allow the status quo, or take my stand for the values I wanted to establish for our racing team.

Now I'm sure you've also faced these same dilemmas, predicaments and Catch-22s when your two worlds collided.

See, when your faith comes into direct conflict with the culture at your workplace, I know you also feel the tug of war between the part of you that wants to avoid conflict, and the part that wants to take a fearless stand for righteousness.

That's why Peter and John can stand as inspiration for us.

They pretty much found themselves in the same dilemma.

When they saw the crippled beggar and heard him beg for alms, they had to decide whether they would be a vessel in the healing of this man or just pass him by.

They chose to be a vessel.

And when a crowd assembled to witness this remarkable event, the two apostles were forced again to decide whether they would tell the crowd about Jesus Christ, or just hold their peace and avoid making waves.

They decided to testify for the Lord!

Total victory for God!

Likewise, when I was confronted with the mindset of a world that was very different from the church world I knew so well, I was forced to choose whether I should define the ethos for the men on my racing team, or just mind my own business and avoid any possibility of discomfort and conflict.

I chose to do the hard thing.

The uncomfortable thing. I chose the God-thing.

Although I must confess:

I wasn't really thinking about Peter and John that day.

I wasn't trying to emulate the actions of any Biblical hero.

I was just going about my business, like all ordinary men, when I suddenly found myself in a place that demanded a choice.

A stand.

A situation that pumped me full of instant tension between my faith and my personal comfort.

Like Peter and John, I didn't want to offend anyone. But a real Christian doesn't just stand by and approve of things through his silence. He gets involved, and intervenes, not allowing the status quo to prevail.

So I did what Peter and John did.

I spoke up.

Not because I was inspired to follow in their footsteps!

Or because I knew I had the answer to the situation at hand!

I spoke up because *I had to.*

Something inside me said, "Jeff, you gotta stay strong. Don't just stand there and bite your tongue!"

It was the Holy Spirit.

The same Holy Spirit that stirred Peter and John to take a stance on that day is the same Holy Spirit who prompted me to challenge the guys on my team not to default to their normal run of the mill response to difficulty.

Under pressure, the Holy Spirit drove me to my own default setting. *My faith.*

The believer who would win people to Christ is the believer who must learn, sooner or later, to take risks in exercising his faith.

Personally I can't think of a miracle that happened in the Bible when people were just sitting around in safety and security. Can you?

I can't think of a miracle that occurred when people were just lounging and chilling out in their La-Z-Boy chairs in their comfort zones of predictability.

But every time the people of God took *bold steps of faith* outside their comfort zones, look what happened:

God always matched their faith with glorious demonstrations of His power!

God parted the Red Sea for Moses—because Moses painted himself into a corner while doing what God told him to do.

God gave David a great victory over Goliath—because David was unwilling to just stand around and cower in fear like the rest of the Israelite soldiers while a heathen giant slandered the name of the Lord.

God directed the ravens to feed the prophet Elijah during a great famine in Israel—because Elijah dared to get in the face of King Ahab and confront him with the truth.

And God stopped the rotation of the earth—*He stopped the earth's turning!*—and made the sun stand still in the sky for Joshua—because Joshua was willing to engage his enemies in a do-or-die battle.

Watch and see how God matches faith with His glory, when you stick your neck out, and speak up.

STICKING YOUR NECK OUT

But you'll never see the glory of God's power until you stick your neck out.

You'll never witness a miracle in your life until you take a heroic chance.

You'll never know what God can do *through you*, until the day you dare to step up to the plate and do what needs to be done.

Peter and John did what they needed to do on that momentous day. And God used their faith to heal a crippled beggar, to add souls to the church, and to strengthen and motivate the rest of the believers.

But me? Man, I was trembling inside when I spoke to that member of my race team about his language—but you know what? I did what I knew I needed to do.

And God honored me, just as He honored Peter and John.

From that day forward, people at the track began to let me inside their lives, and share the message of Christ with them. And in just a few weeks, because of that risk-taking faith and the newfound relationship among the rest of my team members, and among the other drivers and crewmembers down at the track, God managed to attract most of the members of my own race team to The Rock Church, where many of them stood up and gave their lives to the Lord.

That's the knocking of opportunity you hear, when God starts banging on your door.

If you know you're doing what God's called you to do, and if you know that God is with you while you're doing it, there will be an

137

unquenchable need in your soul to take bigger and bolder risks with your faith.

Not to show off, though.

Not to make a name for yourself.

But to proclaim the Gospel with boldness.

And to honor the name of the Lord.

CHAPTER 15

UNWAVERING DEVOTION

*T*he *Revved Life* is unconventional.

Those who live it are bold.

They're full of faith, whether they are living the Christian life or sharing the Christian faith.

But *The Revved Life* is also devoted to the Lord, because his faith, his boldness, and his creativity flow from his one-on-one relationship with Jesus Christ, and from his understanding of his God-given purpose.

What is your God-given purpose?

If you're a Christian, your assigned purpose in life has two dimensions: to convince unbelievers to become followers of Jesus Christ (evangelism), and then to help those new believers become a life-giving part of the family of God (discipleship).

The precise pathway you choose to achieve this twofold purpose is between you and the Lord.

Your individual destiny in life will be unique to you and quite different from my destiny—which is why we need to be slow to judge each other's chosen paths. Nevertheless, you and I are destined to end up in the same place, fulfilling the same purpose with our lives.

We exist to win people to Jesus who are far from Him.

That's why, after Peter and John were released from prison, they continued preaching the Gospel in spite of the threats of the Sanhedrin. In fact, the church continued to preach the Gospel, because they were dedicated to the Lord and to the singular mission the Lord had given them.

They were certainly unconventional in their methods of sharing God's Word. They certainly had been bold. And nobody could deny their faith. And over time, they showed themselves to be devoted followers, as they continued to preach with passion whether their listeners applauded them or flogged them.

As a result, the Lord did miraculous things through them, as larger and larger crowds assembled in search of God's healing power. And the church grew and continued to gain popularity among the masses.

So the Jewish leaders did what most leaders do, when confronted by anybody who threatens their control.

They became jealous (see Acts 5:17).

They tried to trash-talk Jesus and the resurrection.

And they had the apostles arrested again.

And when an angel released the apostles from prison that same night, the Jewish leaders had the apostles arrested one more time!

By this time, the Jewish elders must have been getting tired of seeing them. So to drive home their point, and to strike fear in the hearts of the apostles, the elders had all of them flogged. And then they released them for the second time.

Now flogging was really a big deal in those days. It wasn't a simple *spanking* with a big belt. If you remember the story of the crucifixion, you'll recall that Jesus was flogged 39 times with a leather whip that had pieces of bone on the ends of the thongs, so that each snap of the whip would tear pieces of flesh from his body.

Flogging was a serious punishment, and could sometimes cause the death of its victims, who would bleed to death or die of infection.

Believers were often flogged. Paul, for instance, was flogged on multiple occasions. I imagine his back had a lot of scars that bore witness to his suffering.

But this episode in Jerusalem was the first time that Christians were flogged because of their bold insistence on sharing the Gospel. The intent of the Sanhedrin was to make the apostles think twice before preaching the Gospel again in a public place. The Jewish elders also wanted to intimidate the other believers, and to discourage them from joining the apostles in their public ministry.

But none of the apostles died that day. In fact, it seems that they were able to make their way home under their own power. What's more, Scripture says they celebrated and rejoiced along the way.

The Bible tells us that they "left the Sanhedrin, rejoicing because they had been counted worthy of suffering disgrace for the Name" (Acts 5:41, NIV).

I can just imagine these guys, fist-bumping each other on the road after getting beaten and flogged.

And then the very next verse tells us that "day after day, in the temple courts and from house to house, they never stopped teaching and proclaiming the good news that Jesus is the Christ" (Acts 5:42, NIV).

So the apostles failed to get the message.

They failed to back down.

In fact, the beating they took from the Sanhedrin that day seemed to stir their passions and motivate them *even more.*

They seemed almost to *relish the punishment.*

They certainly relished the opportunity to suffer for Christ.

PUMPED UP BY FAITH

Can you picture them?

With bleeding backs, they walked out of the council chambers that day, pumped up because of their faith, and excited that they were counted worthy to suffer for Jesus in the same way that Jesus suffered for them.

Because make no mistake: Jesus had taken a beating for them.

Now they were able to take a beating for Him. And that made them happy.

It made them proud.

It made them feel like their lives had a real purpose, and that the Lord was using them in a significant way.

So they were actually laughing and praising God and high-fiving one another as they made their way back to their homes and to their brothers and sisters in Christ. They were excited to know that their lives and their ministries had made this kind of an impact on their city and their nation.

Their obstacles gave them a glorious opportunity to suffer for their faith.

What about you?

Have you ever suffered as a direct result of your faith, or your testimony?

If you haven't, then let me tell you something that might be a little hard for you to grasp:

You see, suffering is one of the most wonderful and powerful experiences a Christian can have!

There is nothing like it. Really! I'm not saying that it doesn't hurt, because it does. Jesus' back was hurting after He was flogged, and the apostles' backs were undoubtedly screaming after they were flogged.

You'll be hurt, too, whenever you're ridiculed, mocked, rejected, scorned, or persecuted because of your faith and your witness.

But like the apostles' backs, your ego will heal.

What will never change is the spiritual power that you'll experience because of your suffering.

In the kingdom of God, there is a strange and inexplicable connection between suffering and spiritual growth.

And between suffering and spiritual authority.

The Bible makes this clear throughout its pages (see Romans 8:17; 1 Peter 2:20, 5:10).

Whenever we face suffering, it's a chance for God to show up, show off and get all the glory when He conquers it.

But suffering is a test.

Persecution will test your devotion. Suffering will either reveal your lack of devotion, or cause your devotion to grow.

Suffering tests us. But with God, it can't break us.

And that's why living *The Revved Life* is unwavering in our devotion. Over time, the sufferings of life and the persecutions of the world will cause the believing soul to grow up spiritually, to shake off the sins that so easily dog us, and to focus on that, which is important in life and in God's work.

So get *pumped* when somebody laughs at you or makes fun of you for your faith.

Get *psyched* when somebody ridicules your beliefs on his blog.

Get *motivated* when somebody mocks your Christian posts on Facebook.

Get *fired up* when you get a bad review on Google because of your fire for the Lord.

The person who's living *The Revved Life* is the person who doesn't shy away from the world's rejection—but actually *expects it* and *welcomes it*, because he understands its source.

He pushes on in spite of it, realizing he can't win every lost soul to Christ, but happy that he's able to win many and to impact many others who will eventually come to Christ later in their lives.

TAKING THE HITS

Devotion is a sign of maturity.

Devotion is a sign of true belief.

Nobody sticks with a belief system that he questions or doubts. And nobody abandons a belief system that he deeply accepts.

So get out there with your faith, and join the battle!

Do your part—then watch God do His part!

Sure, you may take a hit or two, and you may get a bruise or a few bumps. But the conflict will actually increase your faith and your boldness, and it will teach you to grow up quickly and to exercise your faith effectively.

Few things help you grow spiritually like jumping in and participating in spiritual warfare.

And if your faith is genuine, that warfare will strengthen your resolve.

THEY WERE MISSION-DRIVEN AND UNSELFISH

Christians are a unique breed of people. But I guess you've figured that out by now. Little has changed since the first century.

On the one hand, Christians are individuals. Your faith is a personal matter, between you and the Lord.

But while there is a definite element of individuality to the Christian life, there also is a strong element of community.

As Christians, we aren't just isolated individuals—we're members of a spiritual family.

We're accountable to one another.

We're implored to pray for one another.

To forgive one another.

And to provide for one another's needs.

We've been given great leadership, which has the authority to maintain order in the church and to look out for our individual souls.

We've been given a corporate destiny of evangelism and discipleship, which must transcend each individual's personal destiny.

So we are individuals—but we are also members of the Christian community.

We are individuals in community.

It's the same thing as when an individual family member sets aside his own preferences and his personal agenda in order to take care of the overriding needs of his family.

Another example would be when an American citizen might temporarily set aside his own plans and his own freedoms in order to serve the needs of his country in wartime.

Like them, the individual believer is constantly called upon to surrender his personal freedoms, his time, and even his resources to better the church and advance the Kingdom of God.

Consequently, God's people must be unselfish if we hope to be winning souls and to achieve the primary mission that God has given us as His representatives here on earth.

The members of the early church were certainly unselfish, because they truly saw themselves as a family or community. In fact, in multiple places, the New Testament alludes to this exceptional selflessness among the early members of the church. In Acts 2, for instance, where we read about the birth of the church, we are told, "all the believers were together and had everything in common. Selling their possessions and goods, they gave to anyone as he had need" (Acts 2:44-45).

And later on, after the excitement of revival began to run headlong into the realities of persecution, we see that the same spirit of selflessness continued within the church: "All the believers were one in heart and mind," it says in Acts 4:32-34a. "No one claimed that any of his possessions was his own, but they shared everything they had. With great power, the apostles continued to testify to the resurrection of the Lord Jesus, and much grace was upon them all. There were no needy persons among them."

This attitude of responsibility toward others continued throughout the first century, even after the church expanded and assimilated converts from the Gentile culture. The Apostle John, for instance, writing late in the first century, said, "If anyone has material possessions and sees his brother in need but has no pity on him, how can the love of God be in him? Dear children, let us not love with words or tongue but with actions and in truth" (1 John 3:17-18).

The early Christians were taught to think of themselves as brothers and sisters.

They were taught to think of themselves as children of the same heavenly Father (refer again to 1 John 3:17-18).

So spiritual family ties were important to the first believers, and these ties were reinforced by the writers of the New Testament Scriptures, as was the believer's responsibility to other believers in his actions, his attitude, his service, and his charity.

You see, the Christian life is not about *me*.

It's about *us*, the church.

It's about *Him*, the Lord.

It's about *them*, those who haven't yet heard the Gospel.

Why does God heal sicknesses and work miracles in people's lives? So those people can just suck up all the glory?

No way!

It's so the Gospel can be confirmed as truth to a watching world, and the power of God can be demonstrated to those who don't believe.

Why does God want to bless you and shower His favor upon your life? So you can privately bask in the abundance of God's bounty?

Come on!

It's so that God can bless others *through you*.

That's the reason He blessed Abraham, in Genesis 12:2-3.

And that's the reason He blesses you and me.

HOW WE LOVE ONE ANOTHER

Early in the second century, the emperor of the Roman Empire was a guy named Hadrian.

And since this was the time in history when the church was really growing and expanding, Hadrian wanted to know more about this new, emerging sect.

So he did what most power-hungry emperors do—he sent out a spy, a trusted representative by the name of Aristides, to do a little re-con mission for him, and to learn about these strange new creatures known as Christians.

And so Aristides plugged into the Christian scene. He studied the early Christians and gathered intel on them in their everyday lives.

And having seen them in action, he then returned to Hadrian with a mixed report.

But there's one observation I want to talk about. One that has echoed down through the centuries as perhaps the greatest positive report that the church has ever received.

Reporting to the emperor about the character and traits and nature of these strange Christian people, Aristides said, "Behold, *how they love one another!*"

You see, when we love one another as Christians, and serve one another—

When we maintain an appropriate attitude of submission and humility—

When we live what we preach and preach what we live—

We open the floodgates of blessing upon our lives.

And we bring glory to the Lord!

We also validate God's Word in our lives and cause unbelieving men and women to take note of the things we say.

We become credible.

We become real.

We become effective.

So learn to be unselfish. Take hold of the fact that it's *not all about you.*

God loves you and He cares about every detail of your life. But the big picture of redemption is way more important.

And God will get involved in *your life* to the same extent that you get involved in *His program* and *His game-plan* for saving the world through the preaching of the Gospel.

THEY WERE EXTREMELY FOCUSED

Let me stop for a moment and tell you about Eric.

Eric's one of my primary rivals down at the racetrack. Eric's real competitive and a pretty awesome driver. But there are days when I doubt if I'll ever be able to lead him to Christ.

Eric talks to me sometimes. He'll butter me up, and tell me things he thinks I want to hear.

But Eric's the typical individual who speaks out of both sides of his mouth.

When he's talking *to* me, he tells me stuff about me. He will compliment me. Sometimes he instructs me. He even tells me he's glad I am his friend.

He will say things like how much he respects me.

And how much I mean to him.

But when I'm not around, or when Eric thinks his words won't work their way back to me, he'll let fly a ton of terrible things about me, behind my back.

In addition, he can be downright angry when he's competing in a race. Eric wouldn't think twice about running another driver into the fence to gain an advantage on the track.

Eric's part of a group of guys at the speedway who simply won't respond to me, no matter how hard I try to reach out to them.

They don't have much respect for me either. In fact, these guys seem to go out of their way to make my life difficult.

Not only do they race against me in a different way compared to others, and mock me behind my back, but they also make fun of my faith.

Early in my racing career, these are the guys who would refer to me and my crew as the *"Pass The Plate Racing Team"* because our car had a church logo on it. Good ole *"PTP Racing"* was the joke around the pits. As if we were receiving offerings at church to fund our racecar.

It's ludicrous thinking really.

Full of accusation.

It was hurtful too.

But they thought it was funny.

After years of praying for these men, witnessing to them, and living out my faith in front of them, I don't know if they will ever respond to me.

I don't know if they'll ever come to my church.

I don't know if they'll ever learn to accept me as an equal on the racetrack.

I don't even really know if they like me as a person.

But at some point, when it comes to living *The Revved Life* and the sharing of the Gospel, you just have to be mature enough to realize this one hardcore truth:

Not everybody is going to like what you are doing.

Not everyone's going to give you the respect you deserve. In fact, there's a certain group of people in every environment, who will deliberately work against you when you take a stand for Christ.

These people don't want the Gospel or the whole Jesus-thing to intrude upon "their world."

And they don't want Christian people to be comfortable in their presence, if those Christian people intend to proclaim God's truth.

These people liked things the way they were before you showed up.

They'll do everything they can to get rid of you by making life just as difficult as they possibly can.

CHAPTER 16

WHERE THEY THINK YOU BELONG

As someone engaging your faith at this level, there comes a point when you must face the reality:

That not everyone is going to accept Christ.

And not everyone is going to appreciate what you're doing when you share Christ with others.

Not everybody is going to respond or even passively tolerate your sudden appearance in a little world they used to dominate before you showed up.

Oh, they don't mind you worshipping in your little church down on the corner on Sunday mornings.

And they don't even mind Christians having a couple of cable TV channels, and a few bookstores they can call their own.

But they want you to stay in your box.

Because that's where they think you belong.

They don't want you to come out into the real world and start confronting them with the true condition of their souls.

So they'll oppose you, sometimes consciously and sometimes unconsciously, until you either break under the pressure or just pack it up and leave.

That's why, when you come face-to-face with the co-worker who uses ridicule or torment every time Jesus or the Bible comes up, you just have to keep your focus. When you encounter the neighbor who spreads lies about you, just keep your eye on the ball. And when you come up against the competitor who blatantly cheats so he can get a rise out of you, or the bully who openly threatens you with physical harm, just dig in.

Take your stand.

And courageously focus on your purpose and your message.

You have to keep loving these people. You have to keep doing the right things and saying the right things, leaving the results with the Lord.

Is that hard? You bet it is, buddy!

But sometimes we Christians feel like we have to close the deal. We share the Gospel, and then we get discouraged if we don't see immediate results.

But you know what? God isn't on Facebook, counting up all the instant "likes" He gets.

And I don't have to close the deal.

That's not what God told me to do.

He told me to speak for Him, and to represent Him through my life.

The rest? It's up to Him.

If I want to maintain my sanity, I eventually have to accept the fact that not everybody will pray with me to accept Christ as their Savior. I have to realize that some people will accept me while others will oppose me.

Some will like me while others will detest me.

And some who reject me now will think about it, and give their hearts to Christ later on in life. And others who accept me now may even reject me later.

So my job is just carrying the ball when God hands it off to me. Continuing to plow forward with my message and living consistently for the Lord without giving up or surrendering my assigned turf.

THEY OVERCAME

Have you ever watched a college basketball game?

Particularly an important, do-or-die game between two conference rivals?

When the home team commits a foul, and puts a member of the visiting team on the free throw line, the home team's students sitting behind the backboard go absolutely crazy.

You know what I mean. They start screaming and yelling and jumping up and down, to distract the shooter while he's attempting his free throws. They wave their arms, blow noisemakers, and even hold up obscene signs or offensive posters in an effort to cause the shooter to lose his concentration and miss the shot.

The devil is a lot like these students (my apologies to the students).

He'll do everything he can do to keep the soul winner from winning souls, and living *The Revved Life*.

He'll pull out all the stops, to keep us from sharing our testimonies or God's plan of salvation.

We've already seen how he seeks to distract God's messenger from within, by creating self-doubt in our minds, or bombarding us with a sense of unworthiness or incompetence.

But when the internal oppression of the enemy comes up short, he will quickly resort to external means of distracting us from our goal.

That's why it is so critically important for those living *The Revved Life* to stay focused on the main thing, the main purpose to which God has appointed us.

The members of the Sanhedrin tried to distract the apostles from their appointed mission. The Jewish elders tried to frighten the apostles, intimidate them, and get them to back down in their efforts to proclaim the name of Christ throughout Jerusalem.

And what the members of the Sanhedrin could not achieve through direct intimidation, Satan attempted through action that's more coercive.

Satan sought to distract the apostles by creating suspicion among the people, toward their unconventional approach to ministry. He sought to distract the apostles by creating division within the church over the church's efforts to feed its growing population of widows.

But the elders wouldn't respond to any effort—internal or external—to deflate their enthusiasm or distract them from their heavenly purpose.

They ignored the physical threats of the Sanhedrin.

They also accepted the fact that some people wouldn't respond to their message, in spite of its truth.

And they accepted the fact that others would actually go out of their way to oppose them, and to persecute them.

Saul of Tarsus, for example—who later became the Apostle Paul—is a great example of the kind of person who resisted the Gospel. In fact, Saul of Tarsus is the *perfect* example of what I'm talking about, because it took time for God to get through to this hateful man and to impact him with the Gospel.

Meanwhile, the apostles remained calm, continued with their message and kept their focus.

They overcame the threats.

They overcame the dangers, and the hardships.

You should keep your focus too.

In your efforts to tell people about the Lord, or to introduce them to the things of God, keep your eye on the ball and refuse to be pulled off course.

Maintain a laser-like vision, and never take your eyes off the prize.

Stay obedient to God.

When the apostles were threatened, and the Jewish elders commanded them to stop preaching and working miracles, Peter and John replied:

"But Peter and John answered and said to them, 'Whether it is right in the sight of God to listen to you more than to God, you judge. For we cannot but speak the things which we have seen and heard'" (Acts 4:19-20, NKJV).

Follow the example of the apostles, by telling people about the things *you* have seen God do, and the things *you* have heard Him speak into your life.

REFUSING TO BE MOVED

You should also develop another side to your personality.

The side that's not so gentle.

The side that's more resilient.

The side that digs in, and refuses to be moved.

Jesus showed this side of His personality when He cleared the temple of the merchants and the moneychangers, in Matthew 21:12-13.

Peter and John showed this tough-as-nails side of their personalities, when they made it clear to the Jewish elders that their authority ended where God's commands began.

You, too, need to draw a line in the sand, and be willing to fight for the turf that God's given to you.

Just as the Jews of the Old Testament were willing to fight to gain control of the Promised Land, you should be willing to take a stand and fight for the office, the classroom, the laboratory, the fast-food restaurant, or the racetrack that God has promised to you.

There definitely is a warfare aspect to the Christian life, especially when you have invaded the enemy's turf.

No matter where God chooses to place you as His representative, I can positively guarantee you that the devil will raise up at least one ornery soul who will seemingly devote his entire life and every waking minute to making you miserable and making your life hard.

This person will spread lies about you.

They'll do illegal and immoral things to interfere with your work.

They'll taunt you.

And they'll tempt you.

And they'll even threaten you with violence.

At first, this person's efforts will be subtle.

Indirect.

Subversive.

Over time, however, your adversary will no longer be able to restrain his outright contempt for you.

He'll attack you openly and boldly, and stare you right in the eye while he does it.

And if the conflict starts affecting the workplace, your employer may come down on you harder than he comes down on your oppressor.

Don't you love it?

Seriously, when it comes to spiritual warfare, you can easily find yourself fighting against the whole wide world.

But take heart! If you are doing what God destined you to do, the Lord is on your side.

You just have to stay focused.

And you have to be willing to do whatever it takes to deal with these kinds of people.

You have to continue loving them, of course.

You have to continue praying for them.

You have to continue inviting them to church, and demonstrating the reality of the Gospel through your life and your attitudes.

You have to continue telling yourself that these people are obstructing your efforts for a reason.

There's something deep down inside of them that is compelling them to do what they are doing to you. Either the enemy is really afraid of you, and he wants to silence you, or your oppressor is being affected by your witness and he wants to neutralize you before you get through to him.

Either way, you need to stay the course. That's what the apostles did, and that's what the Lord wants you to do.

He wants you to remember how He has changed your life and destiny, and He wants you to tell people how He can change their lives and destiny too.

Believe me, if you just keep on keeping on, every person in your sphere of influence will eventually have a day when he'll open his heart to hear what you have to say.

That's when you can seize the moment to tell that person how God has changed you. How He has changed the circumstances around you. How He has changed the course of your life.

You can tell that person how you became a better husband.

Better wife.

Better father.

Better mother.

Better leader.

Better worker.

Or better person, because of your life-changing encounter with the Lord.

HOLD YOUR POSITION

When it comes to spiritual warfare and the opposition you'll experience as you start living *The Revved Life,* I wish I could stop here and tell you things would be easy.

I wish the Sanhedrin were your only problem.

I wish the bully at work was your only opponent.

Unfortunately, most of the resistance you'll get in your efforts to win souls will come not from adversaries in your workplace, but from the people of God *in your own church!*

It will come, not through the direct attacks of the unbelieving, but through more subtle opposition from your own brothers and sisters in Christ.

That's one way Satan wages war, using the church as a battlefield.

Maybe in your church you've experienced something similar.

Not long ago, I was driving behind the pace car in the warm-up laps before a race. I had been the fastest qualifier for this particular race, so I was sitting on the pole position that day, waiting for the green flag.

To my right, on the outside, was the second-place qualifier. As we were making our final warm-up lap in anticipation of the green flag, I knew what my job would be.

My job as the lead qualifier would be to do everything possible to *hold my top position* going into the first turn of the race.

I knew that the second-place qualifier was going to do everything in his power to take the lead away from me. And I knew that I had to keep him high on the track, to my right, so he couldn't gain the advantage and pass me at the start of the race.

In other words: my job was *to hold my position*, but his job was to *put me out of position*, so he could take control of the race.

Later on, I gave some thought to this common racing scenario. And once again, I saw the tremendous parallel between the racing world and the spiritual world.

What the second-place qualifier wanted to do to me at the start of the race is exactly what Satan wants to do to me *all the time!*

He wants to put me out of position so I will lose the race.

He wants to gain the upper hand in the battle I'm waging to establish a place for Christ in the racing world.

But what really makes me sad as I think about it is the fact that most of the people the devil uses to knock me out of position are *Christian people.*

Not those far from Jesus!

The enemy constantly uses ignorant, narrow-minded, but well-intentioned believers to distract us from our mission, and from the prize of winning souls.

In the same way that Satan used Peter to try and take Jesus' focus off His primary mission in life, in Matthew 16:21-23, so Satan uses uninformed believers to try to deter us from completing our assignment.

This goes back to my first premise in this chapter.

To be an effective soul winner, you have to take an approach to ministry that is unorthodox, an approach that many people may not accept or understand.

The old, tired, worn-out methods of evangelism may be more agreeable to Christians who haven't talked with someone about Jesus in 20 years. But if you really desire to penetrate the darkness and enter the world of those searching for truth you need to reach, you have to do something that might offend the religious establishment.

Jesus offended the religious establishment all the time!

He ate with sinners.

He forgave prostitutes.

He hung out with liars and adulterers and lepers and perverts.

He healed people on the Sabbath.

He did all kinds of things that upset the Pharisees and the Sadducees!

He spoke about change from within. He proclaimed a new birth, not just external adherence to a bunch of religious rules.

It was the religious people of His day that offered Jesus most of the resistance He faced. Most of His opposition came from those who should have been His most ardent supporters and His most faithful allies in the spiritual battle for the souls of men.

But that's always the way for the man who tries to live the way we are talking about in *The Revved Life*.

Reaching people far from God triggers opposition.

If you are effective, you'll usually stand alone, and you may find yourself spending more time fighting Christians than unbelieving people. That's why King Solomon noted, "He who wins souls is wise" (Proverbs 11:30, NKJV).

But the man who wins souls is also rare.

He's rare in the church, and he's rare in the world.

He's also a threat.

He's a threat to the religious elite. "We've always done it *this* way," they'll say.

And he's a threat to the kingdom of darkness. "Who do you think you are, coming in here and telling me how to live my life?" they'll stand and accuse, "I've been working here longer than you've been alive!"

Here's the deal: the road to living *The Revved Life* is paved with challenges.

But on that road, God will bless you, encourage you, inspire you, and guide you.

But it won't be easy.

CHAPTER 17

PRESSING THE ESCAPE KEY ON YOUR OLD LIFE

After Jesus was gone and the apostles were on their own, they endured a lot of mistreatment.

They dealt with challenges to their ministry. They took a lot of abuse and persecution from unbelievers. But, in the end, they did the right thing.

They dealt with the distractions.

And then they returned to their principal mission.

They stayed focused, and refused to let believers, unbelievers, or the demons of hell deter them from their assigned purpose.

They ran their race.

And they ran it well.

And that's why the church grew and the entire world eventually heard about the Lord.

The Bible tells us: "Day after day, in the temple courts and from house to house, they never stopped teaching and proclaiming the good news that Jesus is the Messiah" (Acts 5:42, NIV).

They wouldn't give up.

They just wouldn't quit.

They were the most stubborn, obsessed, resolved, insistent, determined, obstinate bunch of people the world had ever seen.

Why shouldn't they be? They had seen and heard incredible things that changed their lives forever. These guys could never be the same—and they could never behave with the indifference and apathy they'd shown before they met Jesus.

My prayer is that you'll do the same thing.

Press the "delete" key on all your old apathy.

Press the "escape" key on your indifference.

Grab hold of the new life—*The Revved Life*—that Christ has offered you.

Hang in there, and keep your eye on the ball. The ballpark will be filled with a lot of distractions.

Announcers will be announcing.

Lights will be flashing.

Music will be blasting.

Vendors will be peddling food and souvenirs.

And people will be screaming and cheering at the same time.

Some will be cheering for *you*.

But if you are a member of the visiting team in some other team's ballpark, most will be mocking you, and jeering at you, and yelling at you, because they don't have anything better to do with their time.

And you'll be a direct threat to the outcome they seek for the game.

Right now, at this moment, the whole game comes down to you.

You're the guy under the bright lights. You're the guy at the plate. The guy with the bat in his hands and the bases loaded and your team down by a run.

You can either lose it all or win it all, on a single swing.

So as the pitcher winds up and releases the ball and sends his best change-up flying your way, you have to do what nobody else in that ballpark is doing.

With unimaginable focus and with intense concentration, you have to keep telling yourself what you want to do with that pitch.

Stay focused on the seams of that baseball.

Swing hard.

And knock it out of the park.

You have to shut out all the movement, all the sights, all the sounds, and all the distractions that are intentionally designed to thwart you from your mission.

You have to concentrate on taking your best swing and slamming it into the center of that baseball.

That is your only purpose.

That is your sole assignment in life.

And in your place of ministry, you have to be the guy at the plate who finds broken people and brings them into God's Kingdom.

You have to be the one who's willing to spend the currency of your life—not in pleasing men, but in reaching people for God and making disciples for Him.

That's your purpose.

That's your assignment.

That's your mission.

That's your driving force.

That's the profile of a winning soul.

Do it well.

PART 4

THE PRINCIPLES OF *THE REVVED LIFE*

CHAPTER 18
THE LAW OF FORM AND FLOW

Jesus came and told His disciples, "I have been given all authority in heaven and on earth. Therefore, go and make disciples of all the nations, baptizing them in the name of the Father and the Son and the Holy Spirit. Teach these new disciples to obey all the commands I have given you. And be sure of this: I am with you always, even to the end of the age."
— Matthew 28:18-20, NLT

The dictionary defines *principle* as "a fundamental truth or proposition that serves as the foundation for a system of belief or behavior or for a chain of reasoning."

As Christians, if our *system of belief* is that the Gospel is God's solution for man's spiritual needs …

And if our *chain of reasoning* is that God has called His people to share this good news with those who need it …

Then we need to understand the fundamental truths that can guide us as we attempt to act upon our beliefs.

We need to understand the propositions that can direct our steps.

It's one thing to have the desire to live *The Revved Life* and win souls.

But it's another thing to know *how* to do it and to know *why* we must do it.

In *Chapter 13*, I introduced you to the spiritual principle of uniqueness. And, in an effort to make this principle understandable, I referred to it as the *law of difference*. Now, I want to share another spiritual principle with you, another divine law that comes to us through the Word of God.

I'll call it the *law of form and flow*.

In God's created order, anything that has life must also have form.

In other words, in the physical world, the intangible quality of life is always packaged and maintained within a physical body.

This is obvious when we look at human beings.

All human beings have bodies. And the life within those bodies is the intangible. It can't be seen, touched, weighed, or measured. But that life doesn't just float around in the atmosphere. God packaged that life within a physical body.

This is also obvious when we look at animal or plant life. There's an intangible thing called *life* within all these created things—but the life that God created is contained within its physical package. Thus, the life itself can be referred to as *flow*, and the physical bodies that contain this life can be referred to as *form*.

The *flow* of God's life is contained in a physical *form* and expressed through that physical *form*.

Not only does this principle apply to obvious things like human, animal, and plant life, but it also applies to other created things like energy.

Like electricity.

Electricity, like life, is another powerful force that God placed within His creation. If you've ever seen lightning strike a tree or ever felt the shock associated with touching a metal object after walking across a carpet, you know that electricity is an invisible, intangible force that God placed in His universe.

But electricity became a potent force for good when man learned to harness it and to package it by channeling it through cables and wires and running it directly into our homes and businesses, in order to provide the power we need to maintain our lives.

That's how electricity itself becomes the *flow*. It's the power and the life force.

And the wires, the cables, and the conduits are the *form* that gives this formless power its benefit to our lives.

Here's one more example:

Ink.

Ink is messy.

If you've ever had toddler get loose with a Sharpie, you know that it leaves stains that can never be removed from clothes, carpet, and walls. If you've ever taken notes on your hand, you know ink can leave pigment on the skin for days.

But when ink, the *flow* can be placed within a pen, the *form*, then this messy chemical becomes a beneficial tool. It becomes a real asset to our lives, fulfilling a worthy purpose and providing a needed service.

God's world is full of examples we could use to explain the *law of form and flow.*

Simply stated, this law says that God has provided us with many things, from nuclear power to chemical combustion. They have the potential to enrich or improve our lives, or make life easier, better or more enjoyable. But until we learn how to harness and channel these things, until we learn how to take them in their raw form and convert them into manageable systems, they will be more destructive than helpful.

But contained in a proper *form,* all these things become useful to our lives.

They become constructive.

They become tools that can make our lives better, enabling us to enjoy the purpose for which these things were created.

Electricity is the *flow*. But wires are the *form* that enables us to harness the electricity and use it.

Ink is the *flow*. But the pen is the *form* that enables us to harness the ink and use it.

God provides the *flow*.

The power.

The life.

But He expects man to design the *form*.

The tool.

The device.

This is why God told Adam and Eve to subdue the earth and rule over it (see Genesis 1:28). God put everything in the earth we would need for our lives—but He expects us to find it, understand it, and harness it in order to make it work for us, in order to make it productive.

This applies to everything we do, including Bible study.

The Word of God is the *flow*. It's the power of God and the life of God. Its truth can make us free.

But God doesn't just pour His Word into our minds through osmosis. We can't put a Bible under our pillows at night and expect to know every verse by heart in the morning when we rise.

No way!

We have to read it.

Study it.

Apply it to understand it.

We have to extract it and then put it in some sort of order so we can create the *form* that we need in order to understand it.

Memorize it.

Teach it.

And live our lives according to it.

So God gives us the words of life. But He expects us to formulate those words into the guiding principles that will serve as the spiritual compass for our beliefs and our resulting actions.

CHAPTER 19

POPPING THE HOOD ON THE SIX PRINCIPLES

L et's get cranking on something else, too.

Because the time has come in this book to lay down some guiding principles for those of us who desire to live *The Revved Life*. We've already examined the *flow*.

We've talked about the God-given compulsion to win souls. In the same way people feel the call to enlist in the Marines, to serve a cause greater than themselves; this is the force we experience when Jesus Christ transforms our lives.

We've talked about the Biblical mandate to share the Gospel and make disciples. This clarion call found in the words of Jesus is not something a Christian can ignore.

We've also talked about the personal experiences of the disciples as they attempted to win souls in first-century Jerusalem. Their story is compelling.

So we've seen the power.

And we've witnessed the driving motivation.

And we've explored the spiritual energy that determined the early believers and drove them to tell others about Christ, and to walk the Christian walk, even in the face of persecution.

We've even delved into my own personal experiences and impetuses in embracing the place God set me in.

So now, let's hit the brakes a sec, and talk about what's under the hood in this next part of *The Revved Life* ...

It's the *form.*

You remember I said that anything created by God which has life must also have a physical form?

I want to concentrate on the six guiding principles that can help us give *form* to God's *flow.*

I believe there are six principles that can enable the modern Christian to successfully navigate the carefully defended waters of the unbelieving world.

Let's look at these briefly, one by one.

For now I'll hold off talking about theology, strategy, and process. We'll discuss these in the final chapters, where I'll explore the theology behind our message, the strategy for finding and winning those who are open to the Gospel, and the step-by-step process of leading an unbeliever to Christ.

For now though, I want to focus in on the six principles that can help us give *form* to God's *flow.*

The six principles that can help us take our desires, our enthusiasm, and our passion for Christ, and channel them into a meaningful and productive approach to ministry that can truly impact others' lives.

But how do we actually do this, in the modern world?

How do we fulfill this Biblical command to win lost souls and to make disciples?

How do we do this in a media-driven, overloaded and overdosed, Facebook and Twitter-saturated culture that is largely jaded against the Gospel, culturally predisposed to rejecting it, and often mindlessly conditioned to resist it?

What are the steps we can take to break through these barriers, and go on offense when it comes to sharing Christ?

CHAPTER 20

PRINCIPLE ONE: LESS IS MORE AND MORE IS LESS

To understand this spiritual concept, let's go back to the physical example of electricity.

Remember, the same God who created the spiritual world also created the physical world. So the principles that apply in the physical world also apply in the spiritual world.

In fact, the spiritual world was created first. So the things we see and experience in the physical world are merely reflections of the realities that exist in the spiritual world.

Keep this in mind as we examine some of the qualities of electricity.

Electricity, if unharnessed and uncontrolled, causes more destruction than it does good.

Many of the world's forest fires, for instance, are caused by lightning strikes.

Lightning also kills about 55 Americans each year. Many other people are killed by downed power lines following hurricanes, tornadoes, and other natural disasters. Unbridled electricity is a deadly and destructive force.

Likewise, nuclear energy can be a deadly force.

Most of us either remember or have been told of the horrible tragedy in 1986 at the nuclear power plant in Chernobyl, in the Soviet Union.

According to one report, 200,000 people would die prematurely because of the meltdown of that facility.

But when harnessed, controlled, and directed, both electricity and nuclear energy can be great blessings to the human race.

These forces can heat our homes.

Run our factories.

Power our schools and hospitals.

Electricity and nuclear power drive the engines of commerce. Without them, we'd still be burning coal in our furnaces and chopping wood for our stoves.

These two natural forces, designed by God, are wonderful examples of the concept that less is more and more is less.

God made electricity.

God made nuclear energy too.

But He left it up to man to discover these powerful forces—to learn about them, to harness them according to God's directive, and to use them effectively to do what they were created to do.

In the same way, God also designed the plan for salvation, and He sent His Son into the world to purchase our redemption and execute this plan.

Then He sent the Holy Spirit to empower His people to tell others about Christ and about God's plan of redemption.

God also left it up to the members of His church to figure out exactly *how* to approach people and *how* to present the Gospel to them.

He left it up to His people to understand His call upon their lives to bear witness to Him.

Like harnessing electricity and nuclear power, people have to learn to harness the power of the Holy Spirit in their lives, and to present the Gospel in a way that is palatable.

Understandable.

And attractive to those who hear it.

HATE PREACHING IS GETTING IN OUR WAY

God is breathtaking.

Take a deep lungful. Let that thought roll around in your heart and fill your veins.

I believe it's impossible for a sane person to reject God when God is presented to him in a way that he can relate and understand God's heart.

But too often, the people of God get in the way of their own efforts to represent God to others.

Too often, the people of God go too far and do too much. They feel the whisper of the Holy Spirit has to become an all-out shouting match. So their *more* effort actually results in *less* belief on the part of unbelievers.

Let me explain through another analogy.

Take the idea of owning your own business.

If you own a business, and want to hire a new salesperson to promote your products, would you hire someone who represents you well or someone who offends people by his appearance, his language, or his attitude?

Okay, obviously you would hire someone who represented your company in a positive manner. Right? You probably wouldn't hire someone with poor hygiene or offensive mannerisms. You wouldn't hire someone who was crude or belligerent with his language. And you wouldn't hire someone who disliked the people he'd be approaching with your products.

You wouldn't want that person's bad habits or bad behaviors to get in the way of potential sales.

Like it or not, the people out there in the marketplace are going to judge you and your company by the person who represents you.

It's no different with the Gospel. Christians try and discount their offensive mannerisms, as if they have no impact on the people far from Jesus. Let's be honest, if a Christ-follower can't get through the front door of someone's heart they're not invited!

Listen.

God loves everybody.

He loves every person who belongs to Him.

But just because He loves you and accepts you as you are, that doesn't mean that you are an effective representative for Him.

Don't go throwing this book down with those words. I realize this is a tough truth for a lot of Christ-followers to accept, but stay with me. *The Revved Life* will make you a *more* effective witness for Christ with *less* effort.

God's *product* is the Gospel.

He invented it.

He's the entrepreneur.

Founder.

He paid the price to make it a reality.

And now He wants the whole world to have a chance to try it and to acquire into it.

And when God's *salespeople* go out to present this wonderful product to those who desperately need it, God doesn't want His *salespeople* to become an obstacle.

He doesn't want people to zero-in on the *salespeople*.

I am not the focus.

We are not the lead actors.

Jesus is.

We are in a supporting role. We are not to be the distraction.

The Gospel is to be the focus.

He wants the potential *customer* to give all his attention to the *message*.

Not the messenger.

That's why less is more and more is less.

When you and I go overboard in our efforts to draw attention to the Gospel, we usually fail to draw attention to the Gospel at all.

Instead, we end up drawing attention to *ourselves*.

When a person takes a megaphone to a major sporting event during the rush of people coming and going from the stadium, and starts telling people that they should "turn or burn," this doesn't attract many people to the Lord.

This doesn't showcase the benefits of the *product* we're offering.

The beautiful Gospel.

Instead, this kind of activity turns people off and turns them away from the Lord. The *target* audience is at the game for a good time. They are not thinking about their worldview. So why stand on the corner yelling the Christian version of obscenities at people who are obviously not listening?

I know why. It sells books.

It makes for good stories.

But most of all …

It draws attention to the *salesperson* rather than the *product*.

It makes unbelievers think all Christians are a few fries short of a Happy Meal.

And that's a foolish and ineffective way to win souls for Christ.

Those who do such things usually do them for one of two reasons.

First, people do bizarre things in the name of the Lord in order to feel good about themselves and to feel like they have *suffered for Christ.*

But they haven't *suffered for Christ!*

Instead, they've suffered as a direct result of their own strange behavior, which deserves the reproach of people.

So no crowns will be distributed in heaven for this kind of self-serving activity.

Second, people do bizarre things in the name of Christ to impress their best buddies in their own little segment of the Christian world. There are some guys who believe that spirituality is somehow synonymous with bizarre behavior. This is a subtle form of pride and self-righteousness.

C'mon, people!

These kinds of things don't do anyone any good.

They don't honestly represent the Lord.

They don't attract people to Christ.

They don't glorify God.

And they don't point people to Jesus.

These kinds of activities do more harm than good.

Like unbridled electricity or unrestrained nuclear power, they leave a lot of destruction in their wake, and usually require a subsequent cleanup effort by those who hope to share the Gospel responsibly with these same people later on.

Now for my disclaimer. I am certain someone who deploys this practice will tell me story after story about the "one here" and the "one there" who actually did give their life to Christ. And for that I am truly grateful. God is smiling.

But don't forget this method usually filters through 20-30 thousand people who walk away empty and confused with a distorted view of Jesus, the Gospel, and Christians for every 2-3 who maybe make the decision on the sidewalk.

And I would guess the majority of those who do respond are not new conversions like Christ and the early Apostles experienced, but more likely people already familiar with the Gospel returning.

Or they're drunk.

Hate preaching is over for now. It worked in generations past, but today it's the clanging cymbal.

THE JESUS APPROACH | IT'S PERSONAL

Jesus had an amazing ability to share the Gospel with people.

Sometimes, He preached to the crowd, and sometimes He worked miracles that caused the masses to stop in their tracks and take notice of Him.

He could be brutally honest and He could be unbelievably forgiving.

He could be passionate.

He could be loving.

He could *touch.*

He could *connect.*

But the best sermons Jesus ever preached were sermons He preached to people like Nicodemus or the Samaritan woman at the well (whose name was never recorded).

These were personal conversations, held in the strictest privacy so that nobody could hear what was being said except Jesus and the one to whom He was speaking.

In past generations, when street preaching was more effective and more socially acceptable, it may have been an effective way of reaching unbelievers for Christ.

But in this day and age, when people are hungry for more substance and less show, for more truth and less criticism, the more personal approach to soul winning is typically the most effective.

The reason Jesus was able to speak to powerful and important people such as Nicodemus, and just as easily to unknown and obscure people like the Samaritan woman, is because of one thing:

He was so *approachable.*

Unlike the person who goes overboard with excessive displays of weird antisocial behavior, Jesus was extremely normal.

He wasn't freakish.

Or eccentric.

He was just a normal guy.

He was a human being.

He didn't stick out like a sore thumb or a neon sign.

Unlike John the Baptist, who screamed at the crowds and wore funny clothes (he had a totally different mission in life), Jesus blended in naturally.

In fact, the Bible tells us on several occasions that Jesus didn't stick out in any way. He was as normal and common as you could get in His appearance and demeanor.

That's why the residents of Nazareth, who watched Him grow up, were unwilling to believe that He was the long-awaited Messiah.

Jesus was too much like them.

He was *too normal!*

So Nicodemus felt comfortable talking to Jesus in the middle of the night about his spiritual questions.

And the Samaritan woman felt comfortable talking to Jesus about her past moral failures and the current state of her spiritual life.

You see, Jesus had a way of *listening.*

He had a way of *accepting people.*

He never judged people.

Or lectured them about their past mistakes or their shortcomings.

So people just naturally felt comfortable with Him.

They talked to Him.

And as they realized they could trust Him, they shared more and more about themselves with him.

Their darkest secrets.

Their deepest wounds.

Their greatest fears.

Eventually, Jesus pinpointed the greatest need of that individual's life, and He fashioned the presentation of the Gospel to match up with the need He discovered in each person.

It's how he got me.

You see, my father was a war hero, but a zero at relationships. Before my father and mother met Jesus Christ (on the same night in different places) my family was a war zone.

Drugs and alcohol were the weapons of our household. Adultery was the largest bomb in the arsenal.

By age 6 I had enough *war stories* to last a lifetime.

If you've seen those environments you know what I mean. I'd wake to people sleeping randomly around my house. Vomit running down the siding from the second floor. It was carnage. Often.

But on June 3rd, 1978, my dad in a jail cell had the Lord approach him, and rolling over on his cot he experienced what Nicodemus had; a personal touch through a very real moment of prayer.

It was 10:30 PM.

I was home sleeping as my mom was trying to figure out her life. But at 11:45 PM Jesus met Mom while she kneeled by her bed just like the Samaritan woman.

And just like that my destiny changed! I'd follow in their footsteps and spend the rest of my days knowing Jesus Christ.

It's that personal.

He is that interested in our story.

That's what makes Jesus so attractive.

NEED A START? | FIND A NEED AND FILL IT

Ruth Stafford Peale, the wife of Rev. Norman Vincent Peale, used to say that the driving motivation behind successful ministry was to "find a need and fill it."

That's exactly what Jesus did.

And that's what you and I must do, too.

We must find a need.

And fill it.

But the truth is, nobody's going to share their heart and soul with a stranger.

Nobody's going to open up to us, on Day One.

So, *Revved Life* effectiveness begins with the building of relationships.

It begins with the creation of trust.

It begins by blending in with people in the healthy areas of their lives, and putting a respectable boundary up to protect oneself from the unhealthy behaviors in their lives.

Find the touch points of what you have in common with people.

Where you connect.

And build a foundation of trust on that.

Forge a relationship.

Build a bond.

Create a connection.

Over time, people will begin to recognize that you're different. They'll begin to recognize that your actions, your attitudes, your words, and even your work ethic are worth noting. They'll begin to see that you are genuinely happy.

And that the important things in your life are set in order.

And that your priorities are producing good things for you.

DON'T TRY SO HARD

As people get to know you, something strange and divinely beautiful will happen.

They'll open up.

And they'll start sharing things about themselves with you.

And as you accept them and show love and respect for them, they will trust you with more, eventually providing you with a wide-open door to introduce them to Christ.

Once you know the deepest need of a person's life, you know how God can meet that need. You can share with them what the Bible says about that need.

You won't need to force it.

Or coerce.

It'll be natural.

Better yet, you can simply tell the person what God has done in that area of *your* life.

You can be vulnerable.

You can be truthful.

You can identify with the individual, and share with him the things you've seen and heard, just as the apostles did.

But if you start sticking gospel tracts in somebody's face, or telling him all about hell and the end of the world with a deranged look in your eyes, that person is going to think one thing real quick.

You's crazy.

And with good reason! You *IS* crazy.

Seriously, folks, that's not the way Jesus won the hearts of people! And that's not the way He won your heart.

Remember? He won your heart by touching the deepest need in your life with His love. He administered care to your greatest wound and brought His solution to your problem.

He won you with a message of hope.

Trust.

Faith.

Let's drop the politically-correct "spin" for a moment, and be honest here: There's absolutely no reason to be religious or dramatic. Those things are a real turn-off to people. People don't like drama. They don't like weirdness. They don't respond to lunatics.

Or religious nut-jobs.

Or in-your-face cults.

Too many people believe that the Christian life is a life of self-denial.

Of asceticism.

They believe Christians are weird.

Fanatical.

Arrogant.

Hypocritical.

And that worshipping the most transcendent person to ever walk the face of the earth is just the tip of the iceberg for our weirdness.

Many believe Christ-followers can't laugh, joke, or have any fun.

People far from God believe the Christian life is more about the things you have to *give up* than the things you *gain*.

They believe the Christian life is boring.

That to follow Christ is to float through life on an imaginary cloud of denial, while ignoring the realities of the world around you.

And why have unbelievers been drinking this Kool-Aid for so long?

Why do they feel this way about Christianity?

Because too many Christians have misrepresented the Lord to them.

Through spewing hate.

Through talking about damnation.

Through denouncing others.

Through phony spirituality.

Or some bizarre presentation of God's Word.

Just be real!

Fit in!

And be human!

God didn't ask you to stop being human when He saved you, right? He just asked you to stop being a sinner.

So take it easy, and take it natural.

Somebody once said that the best definition of the supernatural life is simply to live a natural life in a super way. And somebody else said that the best definition of the supernatural life is to live a super life in a natural way.

Either way, the foundation of true Christianity is Jesus. Do what he did.

Be natural.

Be real.

Be you.

Don't try so hard.

CHAPTER 21

PRINCIPLE TWO: THE ASK

If you're married, then give yourself a high-five: because you've successfully navigated that special, yet awkward, season of life known as courtship and dating.

You pursued—or you were pursued—and you managed to find a way to not only survive the emotional ups-and-downs that the romantic process can inflict, but also to take your relationship with one special person from a casual thing to a lifetime commitment.

How did you do that?

You did it by asking a series of questions.

I did the same thing.

As a young man, I dated from time to time, just as all young men do.

But when I was a freshman in college, I came home one weekend for a visit.

There she was.

Melinda Bowen was always a pretty girl, but while I was away at college, she'd blossomed into a beautiful and elegant young lady.

Boom!

Hottie!

For me, it was love at first sight. (First sight in a long time!) I really wanted to find a way to get closer to her, so I could reintroduce myself and get to know her on a personal level.

So what did I do?

I asked her out on a date.

Young men and young women both have some awkward things to endure as they grow up and learn to relate to one another. But one of the most difficult responsibilities for a young man is the risky task of asking a girl out for the very first time.

If you're a guy, and you've ever been turned down for a date, you know how horrifying it can be to approach a young lady, particularly one who makes your knees weak, and takes your breath away, and ask her to go out with you to a movie or to dinner.

What if she says, "No?"

What if she says, "Jeff, let me think about it and I'll call you later?"

Nothing is worse than the knots you feel in your stomach when you ask a girl out for the very first time!

But the reason this social rite of passage is so important is because it teaches us the necessity of asking the big question.

If I'd never asked Melinda to go to a movie with me, I would never have married her.

But the courtship and dating phase of my life taught me that there are a lot more questions to ask than just the one about the first date. Even after that first date, I had to take another risk and ask Melinda out … *for the second time!*

This was just as scary! Because her answer to this question would tell me whether she liked me on the first date and whether she thought a possible relationship with me was worth pursuing.

It would tell me whether she'd had a good time with me, and it would tell me whether I'd made a good impression on her.

But the opportunities to ask questions didn't stop after that.

They just kept coming!

Eventually, when I knew I wanted something more than a casual friendship with Melinda, I had to ask her if she would be my girlfriend.

I had to ask her if she wanted to be exclusive with me. And, by exclusive, I mean her and I, and I and her. Mano y Mano. One on One.

Talk about scary!

And then the day finally came when I knew I wanted to marry her. So I had to ask two more, very difficult questions.

I had to ask Melinda's father for permission to marry her. (I believe that real men always ask a girl's father, if the father is available, for permission to marry his daughter.)

Then I had to ask Melinda the same question.

I wish I could tell you that I was cool—

Calm—

Confident—

And collected when I asked all these questions.

Man, I wish I could tell you I was convinced she'd say, "Yes" as each new chapter unfolded. But I wasn't.

I was shakin' in my boots. My brain was spinnin'. I was scared to death. I'm more at ease during a crash at the racetrack than I was when I was asking these pivotal questions of Melinda and her dad.

But those experiences taught me something very important.

They taught me that life is filled with situations that require *the ask*.

We only overcome our fears, when we *ask*.

In the really important matters of life, nothing moves forward until somebody asks a question.

And then somebody else answers it.

UNLEASHING THE ASK

Just think about it!

Do you own a home? If so, you had to make an offer to the owner (*the ask*), and the owner had to either accept your offer or reject it.

Do you have a job? If so, you had to *ask* for the job.

Did you attend college? If so, guess what—you had to *ask* for admission.

Even the simpler, mundane matters of life hinge on *the ask*.

Nobody buys a new car until the salesperson *asks* the customer to sign on the dotted line.

And when I was a teenager I increased my employer's bottom line by simply *asking* the question: "Would you like fries with that?"

Life is risky.

If we don't ask the big questions, we don't get the big responses we seek.

The Revved Life and impacting your world positively for Jesus is the same way.

You can live the Christian life in front of people and share the Gospel verbally every day. But until you finally *ask* a person to make a decision for Christ, and to choose whether he wants to accept Christ as his Savior, all your efforts will be unproductive.

Infertile.

Incomplete.

Likewise, the farmer can plant, fertilize, water, and hoe until the cows come home. But until he actually reaches out his hand and pulls the corn off the stalk, nobody will eat one ear of corn for dinner.

For this reason, I try to fulfill the Great Commission in my life by going into those places where unbelievers reside—such as the racetrack—and developing relationships with them over a long period of time.

The next step? It's waiting for those perfect opportunities to talk to them personally about God and His love for them. And when I get the opportunity to do this, I always conclude my conversation by asking the person something like this, "Are you farther from God than you want to be?"

This question opens a dialogue with a few outcomes. Sometimes the response is, "Yes." And we get a chance to pray right there.

When it works and lands perfectly like that it's amazing. But candidly, that's less of the norm.

Usually, if I can't ask that question, I at least ask him to attend church with me. And this is most often the gateway for transformation. Having a healthy, strong, vibrant church to be connected to is vital! It takes a great restaurant for a chef to serve her recipes to many gathering people, and it takes a great church for a Christian to serve Jesus to the many hungry people.

Sometimes I miss it. I sense it's time to ask the question and it lands awkwardly, then my invitation to Church is met with resistance. It happens. Take the pressure off and keep going forward.

SHAKING IN MY BOOTS AND SWEATING BULLETS

Is it hard to ask this question?

Absolutely!

Every time I pop the big question to a person at the racetrack or the ballpark or anywhere else, I'm shaking in my boots and sweating bullets the same way I did when I asked Melinda out for our first date.

And the same way I did when I took a deep breath and asked her father if I could marry her.

But I knew I had to do it.

I knew I had to dig down deep, find the necessary courage, and then take the risk.

And *ask*.

If I don't ask the most important question that any Christ-follower could ever ask another human being, if I don't seize this opportunity, the person I am addressing won't be able to respond to God's tug on his heart.

This simple question—the question of one's personal decision regarding eternity—is the most important question a person can ever ask.

And it's the single most important question a person will ever answer.

It's the pivot-point in a person's life.

The point at which he will either turn in a new direction, or double down on his worldly beliefs.

Therefore, in living *The Revved Life* my greatest responsibility before God is to make this pivot-point possible.

I am just the fulcrum.

The instrument in God's hand.

If Jesus uses me at this tipping point, I've done what I know to do.

Man oh man!

When the ask works.

There is nothing like it.

CHAPTER 22

PRINCIPLE THREE: UNCONDITIONALLY RELATIONAL

Dan Moore entered his rookie year on the Whelen circuit during my third year as a driver. From the very beginning, Dan came across to me as though he thought he was hot stuff. He appeared to me to be young, cocky, and aggressive. He wasn't super loud, but he was proud and determined he was going to make the point to all us veterans that he was coming through—literally and figuratively (I hope he will smile when he reads this.)

Dan and I really had some squabbles during his first year of racing. He'd run into me on the track, at times when my car wasn't anywhere near his.

There was one time I remember we were racing on a three-eighths-mile track. I was coming off turn 2 when my rear tires were suddenly lifted off the track from behind. I went sliding down the backstretch sideways in front of the entire field. Tire smoke from my sliding tires was pouring into the cockpit, and I was doing everything I possibly could to spin the car out so I wouldn't hit anything. But I ended up hitting the fence—BOOM!—and demolishing my racecar.

It was totally destroyed!

The body panels were ripped off.

The frame was bent.

The suspension was torn apart.

Me? I was fine, but the car was really messed up.

Needless to say, I was very disappointed. I'd already been through a frustrating season, and Dan had crashed into me too many times before this incident. He already announced that he didn't think he had done anything wrong the preceding weekends. He believed that the majority of his incidents were "just a racing deal." Like no biggie.

So now, it's the next weekend. My car is all repaired and we are back at the track for another race day. And Dan comes walking up to me in the pit area.

I admit, I expected the worst. But here he was approaching, thrusting his arm out, extending himself in an effort to shake hands with me.

I have to be honest with you.

I didn't want to shake Dan's hand.

I mean, I know I'm a pastor and everything. And I know I'm supposed to forgive people and show love to them. But that doesn't mean I have to approve of getting wrecked by other drivers or act as if they didn't do anything wrong.

Remember what I told you earlier: Whenever you try to represent the Lord with dignity, there will always situations that'll do everything possible to push your buttons and send you over the edge.

But I was not going to become anyone's punching bag on the track simply because I was a Christian.

So Dan started talking to me. "Jeff, you know what?" he said.

"I had my in-car camera on when we made contact last weekend. I watched the video four times. And all four times, I wrecked you. Sorry about that."

Talk about being thrown a curveball.

I was blown away.

That was Dan's way of accepting responsibility. It was his way of admitting that he'd made a mistake. It went a long way with me.

In any event, his efforts to reach out to me eased the tension between us—not just at that moment, but from that point on. Since then, Dan and his girlfriend, now wife, have been to our church several times.

We're still fierce competitors. We've had some intense battles over the years. In fact, when I won the final race of the 2011 season, Dan and I were the class of the field that day. By the closing laps, he and I were way out in front. I'd been stalking him for 93 laps. Then on the 94th lap, I got underneath Dan, passed him, and went on to win the race.

Dan has since become a good friend. I've found that he is really a great guy. He's won his first speedway championship as of this writing. I respect that greatly. It's hard to do.

It's amazing how relationships can develop when you learn to give and take a little, both on the track and off.

But the really important thing I learned from my developing friendship with Dan is that relationships take time, and they can only be advanced when you become willing to relate to people unconditionally.

THE THREE STAGES OF RELATIONSHIPS

Someone once told me that relationships pass through three stages.

During the first stage, you're in each other's *eyes*. This means that you're watching each other, sizing each other up, and analyzing each other's behaviors. You want to know what makes the other person tick. You want to know what rings his bell.

You want to know how he thinks.

How he reacts to things.

What makes him tick.

What ticks him off.

What makes him laugh.

You want to know if the two of you might be compatible, and if it's really worth pursuing a friendship with that person.

During the second stage of relationship building, you're in each other's *way*. This means that you're getting close enough to each other and spending enough time around each other to start annoying one another.

You start feeling a little more comfortable around the other person, so you start letting your guard down.

You talk more.

You say things you probably wouldn't say to a stranger.

You also are silent more often in the other person's presence.

Silence is an indication of comfort and security. While strangers get nervous around each other during awkward moments of silence, people who are becoming friends learn to be increasingly comfortable in the other person's presence without constantly yakking it up.

In fact, I believe that a true friend is a person you can sit with for ten minutes of complete silence, without feeling anxious and without even noticing the passing of time.

But this stage of relationship building doesn't come easy.

As a man and woman get closer to one another in a developing romance or as two men or two women start building a friendship, they must pass through this stage of relationship building where they feel comfortable letting their guards down.

Then they have to wait and see if the relationship can survive the honesty.

When the other person sees you, warts and all, will that person still like you?

When that person sees your worst side, will that person still want to be around you?

And will you still want to be around *them?*

If a growing friendship survives the first two stages of relationship development, you finally move on to the third and final stage of friendship.

This is where you find yourselves in each other's *hearts.*

This is what it's all about—the core, the essence—and this is possible in every imaginable environment. But it takes time. It requires a lot of give and take.

And it requires complete acceptance of the other person.

UNCONDITIONAL

But while acceptance of a person into the most intimate areas of your life should be *conditional*, acceptance of a person for the purpose of connecting them to Christ must be just the opposite.

Unconditional.

What I mean is, I get to pick my friends, but I don't get to pick who attends my church.

God does that. On any given Sunday morning the Lord will prompt someone to come for the first time. Sometimes He even releases someone to stop coming and go to another church.

My friendship with people is conditional. But my task and calling to people is unconditional. I am called to them.

So are you.

If you want to marry someone or become business partners with another person, your acceptance of that person should definitely have conditions. The Word of God and wisdom itself teach us that we should be careful and discerning about the people we allow into the inner sanctums of our lives. You should be extremely cautious, therefore, in the selection of those with whom you choose to *yoke* yourself with in a way that will enable them to shape your destiny.

But *The Revved Life* is different.

Living *The Revved Life* conditions us to be *unconditionally relational.*

This means that, to be effective, you and I must love people and reach out to them.

Without prejudice.

Without judgment.

When we share Christ we are not trying to necessarily link ourselves to that person for life.

We're simply trying to understand what makes him tick and to let him know that he is loved and highly valued by God. We're trying to find enough common ground with that person to create a starting point from which to help him rebuild his life.

At the start, you just want to have enough trust between you and that person so you will be invited to talk to him about the things that really matter.

That's the way to the heart.

But once you connect at the heart-level friendship is often discovered. Some of my best friends are people I've led to Jesus Christ.

The converse is also true. I hope it goes without saying that the low hanging fruit is often the people you are already friends with. I've spent a lot of time with people who don't possess the same Christian worldview as me.

They are not convinced of the claims of Jesus Christ, yet.

They don't believe like me.

However, I enjoy their company. I enjoy being their friend. And doing rad stuff together.

Candidly, we must see people for what they are, wonderful people in need of love and acceptance. They are not our spiritual science project for salvation. Instead they are brought across our path to interact with us, to get to know us.

And when we live *The Revved Life* there's a good chance our friends will find Christ at the center of it all.

Never forget that.

JESUS NEVER REJECTED

Jesus invited only twelve men to follow Him day by day.

He invited only twelve men to eat with Him.

To travel with Him.

To laugh with Him.

To grieve with Him.

To get to know His family and His mission in life.

It was these twelve men He took aside so He could pour into them His wisdom and His insights.

These were the twelve men He taught to pray and the guys to whom He explained His coming impact on human history.

But Jesus had other relationships on other levels with other people.

Because Jesus was wise enough to know that all relationships aren't the same.

In His life, there were the masses who followed Him so they could see something miraculous happen. They just wanted to see a leper healed or a blind man cured or the lame walk; like Jesus could be standing outside Walmart handing out free miracles.

But there were others.

There were the 500 who saw Him after His resurrection.

There were the 120 who believed in Him strongly enough to return to Jerusalem to pray for ten days while waiting for the outpouring of the Holy Spirit.

There were the 70 He sent out in pairs to preach, heal, and cast out demons.

There were the twelve who abandoned their homes and their occupations in order to devote their lives to Him.

There were the Big Three—Peter, James, and John—whom Jesus took aside to teach special things.

And then there was John, the "disciple whom Jesus loved," who was so close to the Master that he was willing to actually go to Golgotha and stand beneath the cross to personally witness the crucifixion.

Jesus had relationships on all levels.

And He accepted people on all levels.

"Right, Jeff, I get it. But I'm not Jesus. What's your point?" you might be saying.

It's this:

If we want to be effective spokespeople for Christ, we must learn to do the same.

We must learn that there will be very few people in our lives who are worthy of sharing our sufferings.

Or worthy of being entrusted with our innermost dreams.

Or our greatest fears.

But there are tons of people out there in the crowd who still deserve our compassion.

Our best efforts.

And a little of our time and attention.

The thing that was so amazing about Jesus is the fact that He accepted people on all these different levels and He never rebuked or chastised anyone for failing to move up the relationship ladder.

He didn't reject guys who weren't ready to experience a real fellowship with the Body of Christ.

He didn't zing girls for not braving the sea of believers to touch the hem of His garment.

Jesus left it to each individual to decide how close he wanted to be to the Lord.

If a person was content to sit in the back of the crowd and listen to the teachings, and just kick the tires of his belief, Jesus was happy to have that person there.

But if a person wanted to kick things up a notch and become a true follower, Jesus was willing to allow that person to move into His inner circle—provided the person was willing to pay the higher price for increased spiritual intimacy.

As Christians, we need to learn to think like Jesus.

We should love unconditionally.

And we should demonstrate both the love of God and the power of God to anyone who is willing to receive it.

We should also be open to letting new people into our lives, as those people grow and prove themselves worthy of our trust.

But we should never reject anyone.

Not the fallen.

Or the sick.

Or the abused.

Or the burned-out.

The only people Jesus ever rejected were the religious bigots. (I will resist the temptation to comment on this subject.)

THE DOOR IS WIDE OPEN

The promise of salvation is made to "as many as the Lord our God shall call" (Acts 2:39, KJV).

So the door is wide open.

Don't slam it shut.

Don't hammer nails in it by rejecting people or turning away from them.

Jesus loved the Jews and the Gentiles alike. In fact, that's one of the things that got Him in trouble. He healed everyone from lepers to the children of Roman centurions.

He spent time with priests like Nicodemus and outcasts like the woman caught in adultery.

Jesus had no favorites. He saw eternal value and potential in everyone. He knew each served a deeper purpose.

He was unconditionally relational.

CHAPTER 23

PRINCIPLE FOUR: WINNING PEOPLE

W hy do we Christians put so much emphasis on reaching people for Christ?

That's a subject I haven't yet tackled in this book.

I know Jesus told us to preach the Gospel and to make disciples and this command alone should be sufficient to stir the church to action and obedience. But there's a reason *why* Jesus gave this command to His disciples.

There is a reason sharing the Gospel stood at the forefront of the church's activities in the book of Acts.

The Revved Life is not really a theological book. It's more about my personal story of moving from the pits after losing my parents to the podiums of life. It's a book I hope gets you to take action from out of your own metaphorical graves to living a brilliant life with Jesus as your true North.

The Revved Life is about developing a real color picture of Acts 1:8. These final words of Jesus while on earth were the beginning of a way of living.

The Revved Life is that way of living.

Nevertheless, it's necessary for the Christ-follower to know *why* he must reach people for Christ and *why* he must disciple those he wins for the Lord.

Because of the importance of the theological motivations for any book which calls on people to take action on behalf of Jesus, I plan to devote the entire next part to a theological analysis of *The Revved Life*. For now, however, let me just say that the follower of Christ has no option:

He *must* reach people with the Gospel of Jesus Christ.

He *must* testify for the Lord.

He *must* declare the things he has seen God do and the things he has heard God say.

If God truly exists (and He does) and if the Bible is the true revelation of God (and it is), then those of us who follow Christ must start taking this witnessing thing seriously.

We must start taking eternity seriously.

This is not a game.

This is real.

GETTING STRAIGHT

Jesus put everything into perspective when He asked, "What good will it be for a man if he gains the whole world, yet forfeits his soul?" (Matthew 16:26, NIV). That pretty much sums it up!

In the modern church, it's so easy to get caught up in the latest debate over the teachings of prosperity or the proper stance of the church on the issue of gay marriage.

It's easy to get caught up in questions about the appropriate type of music for worship or the proper titles for those who govern and lead the church.

But a million years from now, nobody will remember these so-called pressing issues of the day. Nobody will care. All that will really matter a million years from now is who is present with us in heaven and who is not.

Heaven is real. And hell is real, too. And I know we don't like to think about these things in this current age of positive confession and self-help preaching, but God wasn't kidding around when He said, "Whosoever was not found written in the book of life was cast into the lake of fire" (Revelation 20:15, KJV).

So let's keep our focus.

Let's keep our priorities in order.

I'm not saying that teachings about family life are unimportant.

I'm not saying that worship conferences are unnecessary.

I'm not saying that financial seminars or classes on parenting don't have their rightful place in the church—because all these things are parts of building strong disciples.

But I am saying that everything must take a back seat to our primary task.

And that's *winning. Winning. People. To. Jesus. Christ.*

Because there are no people to disciple, until there are people who believe. If the other activities of our lives interfere with the primary objective of winning people we must set aside those other activities until we can get our priorities straight.

WHAT'S PRIMARY IN THE MIND OF GOD

Listen.

A church is free to do anything it wants to do, as long as that activity isn't strictly forbidden in the pages of God's Word.

An individual Christian is free to do anything he wants to do, as long as that activity isn't forbidden in the pages of God's Word.

God will judge each man according to that man's opportunities.

And He'll judge each church according to the spiritual fruit that the church produces.

But if a church or a person ignores the primary responsibility entrusted to them as representatives of Christ, that church or person has missed the mark and has failed to complete the overriding mission that Jesus gave to His followers.

Some churches build hospitals and colleges. That's okay! That's awesome! There's absolutely no problem with that.

Some churches build homeless shelters and halfway houses. And that's okay and pretty awesome, too! In fact, The Rock Church does its own things to serve the needs of our community.

But here's the ultimate question that God will ask on Judgment Day when He puts every ministry through the fires of His intense scrutiny:

How did this activity contribute to the reaching and winning of people? How did we then disciple believers?

Because, if the hospitals and the colleges feed into this ultimate purpose, and if the homeless shelters and halfway houses contribute to this end goal, then those who contributed to these will be highly rewarded.

And if not, their works will be consumed in the fires of judgment as "wood, hay, and stubble" (1 Corinthians 3:12, KJV).

In the early church, the people took care of one another's physical needs. They were unselfish and willing to share their earthly resources in order to feed those who truly needed it. In fact, the charitable operations of the early church became so massive that the apostles eventually were forced to appoint seven exceptional men, just to manage the food programs of the church.

But it's interesting to note what the apostles had to say when the food program became a problem.

Know what they said?

They said, "It would not be right for us to neglect the ministry of the word of God in order to wait on tables" (Acts 6:2, NIV). So "we will turn this responsibility over (to the seven men you have chosen to oversee this responsibility) and will give our attention to prayer and the ministry of the word" (Acts 6:4, NIV).

The apostles knew what was important: the ministry of the Word to people.

They knew what was primary in the mind of God.

As the successors to these founders of the church, we must also keep our priorities straight.

There are a lot of good and wonderful things we can do—as a church and as individuals—but nothing else really matters unless people hear the Gospel, believe it, accept it, and turn their lives over to God.

And that's what it's all about. The main thing is that we keep the main thing the main thing.

The Revved Life.

CHAPTER 24

PRINCIPLE FIVE: MAKING DISCIPLES

D o you have a coin in your pocket or purse?

Get it out.

I want to show you something.

Take a look at your coin and you'll see that it's engraved on both sides. A dollar bill is printed on both sides, too. In fact, any denomination of currency that's printed or engraved on just one side would not be regarded as legal tender.

Now look closer.

On one side of your coin, there's the likeness of an important figure in our nation's history: George Washington, Thomas Jefferson, Abraham Lincoln, or Franklin Roosevelt. We call this side of the coin "heads."

On the other side of the coin, you'll find the likeness of a national monument.

We call this side of the coin "tails."

"Heads" and "tails" make up a complete coin.

Just as a coin is incomplete and useless unless both sides of it are engraved, so our witness of what we've experienced through knowing Jesus is incomplete unless we fulfill both aspects of the Great Commission He gave to us.

As Jesus was preparing to leave the world and return to His Father in heaven, He said: "Go into all the world and preach the gospel to all creation. Whoever believes and is baptized will be saved, but whoever does not believe will be condemned" (Mark 16:16, NIV).

But on another occasion during this same time, Jesus explained the Great Commission further by saying: "Therefore go and make disciples of all nations, baptizing them in the name of the Father and of the Son and of the Holy Spirit, and teaching them to obey everything I have commanded you" (Matthew 28:19-20, NIV).

So there's one aspect of the Great Commission that deals with preaching the Gospel to the unsaved, but there's another aspect that deals with making disciples and teaching them the commands of Christ.

With this in mind, the best possible definition I could offer for the activity of living *The Revved Life* is "the convincing of people to become followers of Jesus Christ AND be helpful members of the family of God."

Your job as a witness, therefore, is to tell the distant about Christ.

But it doesn't end there.

You must also take those who come to the Lord and gently guide them through the various stages of the Christian life.

Help these new believers establish themselves in a local church.

Teach these new believers about Bible study, prayer, and giving, and all the things that become the building blocks of the Christian experience.

Your job is to integrate new believers into a good local church and to interface with those seasoned saints in your workplace who have already come to know Christ, yet who need encouragement and support and spiritual accountability in their lives.

God has placed you where you are so you can represent Him to everyone.

Those who believe.

And those who don't, alike.

PUTTING MY FAITH IN THE FAST LANE

Scott Ellsworth is the former announcer at the Evergreen Speedway in Monroe. In fact, Scott's one of the premier track announcers in NASCAR™.

As you read this book and try to imagine me doing my thing at the racetrack every Saturday, you're probably able to visualize a lot of the activities at the track.

You can see the racecars and the drivers—

The pit crews and all the activity on the drivers' side of the catch fence—

You probably can hear the sounds of the roaring engines—

And you can smell the fuel—

The hot dogs—

And the burning rubber on the asphalt.

But regardless of what you can "see" or "smell" with your imagination, you may be unaware of the many *people* who make things happen behind the scenes.

The racetrack is my "office." And like most professional worksites, it's made up of a lot of people who do a lot of things that the patrons never really notice. In the racing world, for instance, there are announcers like Scott and people who manage the business operations of the track.

There are people who sell food and people who sell tickets.

There are people who maintain order and provide security.

There are people who stock supplies, people who cook, and people who clean. There are people who prepare and distribute the programs. There are people who park automobiles and direct traffic.

There are also the promoters, officials, and the guys who make sure the various crews are setting up their cars according to the rules.

When I told you that I entered a whole new subculture when I became a racecar driver, I wasn't exaggerating! NASCAR™ is truly a "community." Thousands of people work throughout the industry and I've come to know quite a few of them over the years.

But Scott Ellsworth is definitely one of the best.

Scott's a Christian and when I first met him, his wife was suffering from cancer. So I would ask him, "Scott, how are you doing?" I would ask how his wife Ellie was doing, too.

Sometimes, he and Ellie would be doing great. And sharing the joy of that would get us pumped up and put our faith in the fast lane. Other times, Ellie would be struggling and I was able to divide his sorrows by helping him bear some of his burdens. It's a joy for me to witness to those who don't know the Lord, but it's an equally joyous thing for me to pray with those who do know the Lord and who just want someone with whom they can share the Good Lord in their lives.

Since those early days when I first met Scott, Ellie passed away and Scott has remarried. And even though Scott's never attended The Rock Church, we continue to be good friends. I talk with him every chance I get. I pray with him. I continue to ask him how he's doing, and I continue to multiply his joys and divide his sorrows by simply taking an interest in him, and sharing some of the important events of his life.

BUILDING PEOPLE

It's amazing what happened when I dared to venture outside my own comfortable world, and outside the scope of my staff meetings and church services, to rub elbows with the people of my community.

With people close to God and people far from Him alike.

It's amazing how many people wanted my opinion regarding the important decisions in their lives.

It's amazing how many people wanted my blessing.

It's even amazing how many people wanted me to challenge them in their thinking and their behaviors.

Over the years, I've come to realize that it's not about building The Rock Church. In fact, it's not even about building the Kingdom of God.

It's about building *people*.

By building people, we build the Kingdom.

So it's about helping the people see Christ and respond to Him in the same way I did when I first encountered Him in a personal way. It's about taking those Christians who are out there in the community and helping them grow, helping them to overcome their challenges, and become everything God created them to be.

Sometimes these people will come to church.

Sometimes they won't.

Sometimes I notice that they start attending church later, after I've been a part of their lives for a while, because a seed was planted within their hearts that eventually sprouted and produced something good.

My efforts helped them turn a corner or make a necessary change.

And the seed that was planted gave rise to something good when the inspired Word finally met up with the appropriate circumstances in their lives.

That's how the work I do at the racetrack on Saturdays continues at The Rock Church on Sundays. Everything I do is done to win people and to help those who come to believe grow and mature.

Every time I preach, I give those in the congregation an opportunity to invite Jesus into their hearts. And every time I preach, I try to help the already convinced in my congregation learn how to better live for the Lord and represent Him in the world.

In fact, I try to impart to all the members of my church that they too can have the same impact in their little corner of the world, where they can be most effective for Christ.

I try to help them understand that ministry isn't something *I* do.

It's something *we* do.

I want them to know that ministry isn't something a few people do on Sunday mornings, while the spectators sit and watch.

Ministry is something we *all* do, throughout the week, wherever we go.

Sundays are merely "training day."

It's a team meeting per se.

That's right! To me, the purpose of any church service is to worship God and help Christians grow so they can leave the church service and do the work of the ministry wherever God sends them.

I'm not the minister.

They are the ministers.

I'm just the guy who's entrusted with the responsibility for training them and equipping them to do the work of the ministry.

The work that only *they* can do.

EQUIPPING GOD'S PEOPLE

Where does such a radical idea come from?

The Bible! Where else?

Let me show you.

But first, let me begin by asking you a question. And be careful how you answer. This is a trick question.

How many times does the word *pastor* appear in the New Testament (King James Version)? Without opening it, see if you can guess.

Done guessing?

If you guessed *never,* you are correct!

The word *pastor* never appears in the King James Version of the New Testament!

Yet the church has built an entire branch of theology designed to teach us what pastors are supposed to do with their time. We call this branch of theology "pastoral theology," and you can get a college degree in this field.

But what about the plural form of the word? What about the word *pastors*? Does it appear?

The word *pastors,* plural, appears ... *one time!*

So if we intend to build an entire branch of theology around the subject of pastoral ministry, doesn't it make sense for us to pay real close attention to the only verse where the word *pastors* appears in the New Testament?

Shouldn't we begin building our theology of pastoral ministry by focusing on this lone description of the work of a pastor within the Bible?

In Ephesians 4:11, the apostle Paul tells us that the Lord established five "offices" within his church, in order to advance the mission of the church.

He gave us apostles.

Prophets.

Evangelists.

Pastors.

And teachers.

Then, in the very next verse, Paul tells us exactly *why* God established these various offices. Paul tells us that these five offices were created "for the perfecting of the saints for the work of the ministry" (Ephesians 4:12, KJV).

So who is supposed to do the work of the ministry in the church? The saints! And who is supposed to "perfect" the saints and prepare them to do the work of the ministry? The pastors and the other people appointed by God to pour into the saints on Sundays!

My job as a pastor, therefore, is to equip God's people to do the work of the ministry.

My job is to train and prepare believers to go into the mission fields of the world and impact people's lives for God.

I can't personally touch every individual living in my region.

But guess what? The people who attend my church can!

I can't personally infiltrate the educational arena, the political arena, the business arena, and the financial arena of my community. But there are people sitting in my congregation whom God has strategically placed in each of these arenas of American life in order to bear witness for Him.

And these people *can* impact people in every nook and cranny of society—if they'll simply be willing to learn, and I can encourage them in their efforts.

UNTIL UNBELIEVERS BECOME BELIEVERS

You, too, have a unique place of assignment.

You have a purpose where the Lord's planted you, to witness for Christ and to represent Him to both believers and unbelievers.

But you need to know how to do that.

You need to have the tools to do it.

And that's where I come in and where other pastors and teachers come in.

That's where this book comes in.

As a pastor, I have two jobs. My first job is to be a witness in my own life, in the place where God has planted me. But my second job is to teach others to do what I do. And that should be the job of every pastor.

The Great Commission is not fulfilled until unbelievers become believers.

And then not until believers become people who win people.

So devote yourself—not just to church attendance and giving and tithing and serving at your local place of worship. But commit yourself to people.

And to preparing others to win people too, and to be successful in all they undertake for Christ.

CHAPTER 25

PRINCIPLE SIX: TRANSFORMATION

Unfortunately, when all's said and done, all the principles in the world won't help you effectively win people, unless you have a transformed life.

In fact, a transformed life is the best tool you could possess.

If people who knew you *before* you came to Christ can honestly see real changes in you—behaviors, attitudes, priorities, character—they will practically beat down your door to ask you how they can experience this kind of change, too.

In fact, they *will* make a point of asking you that question in a roundabout way.

It's a little like "Show and Tell." Remember elementary school? Every week, you had to bring something to class and stand in front of your classmates and tell them about the thing you brought. The primary purpose of "Show and Tell" was to help you learn how to express yourself, particularly in front of an audience. It was designed to develop your communication skills and to enhance your self-esteem.

But the first few chapters of the book of Acts could also be subtitled "Show and Tell," because the apostles would always *show* the people something before they would *tell* the people something.

In Acts 2, for instance, God sent the Holy Spirit on the Day of Pentecost, and a large crowd gathered to see what all the hubbub was about.

That's when Peter stood up and said, "These men are not drunk, as you suppose. It's only nine in the morning! No, this is what was spoken by the prophet Joel" (Acts 2:15-16, NIV). And then Peter went on to quote Joel and to explain to the people God's simple plan of salvation.

So Peter took advantage of what the people saw to tell them what it all meant.

In the next chapter of Acts, Peter and John healed a lame beggar at the temple gate in Jerusalem. This, too, drew a humongous crowd. And once again, since the people were already "filled with wonder and amazement at what had happened," (Acts 3:10, NIV), Peter seized the opportunity to tell people *why* this happened. "By faith in the name of Jesus, this man whom you see and know was made strong. It is Jesus' name and the faith that comes through him that has given this complete healing to him, *as you can all see*" (Acts 3:16, NIV, emphasis mine).

People can argue with your theology—and trust me, they *will* argue with your theology.

But nobody can argue with your experience.

People can argue about the value of going to church—but they can't argue about the value of something that's changed you from the top of your head to the soles of your sneakers.

So *show* them something before you *tell* them something.

That's what I try to do in my two places of ministry (my church and the racetrack), and that's what you need to do in your place of ministry. Nothing speaks louder and stronger than a transformed life, and the power of the Gospel is demonstrated by what it has done in your life.

ORDINARY BECOMES EXTRAORDINARY

I've seen this phenomenon in action.

The Gospel transforms the ordinary into the extraordinary.

Let me ask you something: Would you buy a product if the commercials offered to make you "ordinary?"

Of course not!

Nobody wants to spend money on a car that gets "ordinary" gas mileage or an attorney who promises "ordinary" results.

Everybody wants the best.

The exceptional.

The cream of the crop.

Even if a person knows deep down inside that he is being hoodwinked, he still wants to go to the business that offers him the "best" or the "newest" or the "fastest" or the "highest-rated."

When the apostles stood before the Sanhedrin, they were supposed to be the *ordinary* people in the room. After all, they were "unschooled."

They had no titles.

No position.

They had zero authority.

It was the guys sitting in judgment of the apostles who were supposed to be the elite people at that gathering.

But the apostles turned the tables on these scholars. The apostles took over the room and commanded the environment and the agenda.

With boldness and confidence and without hesitation or apology, they told the Jewish elders what they'd seen and heard. And nobody in the room could argue with that.

They told the elders the truth about Jesus—and nobody could argue with that either, because deep inside, everyone in that room knew one thing:

That *Jesus was the Christ!*

But it was the dramatic change in the apostles that gave credibility to their message.

And it was the power of God working through the apostles that made the Gospel irresistible.

MERE MEN

Here's the next deal:

Don't try to fit-in too much.

On the one hand, you don't want to conduct yourself as if you're too good for the people you're called to reach.

At the same time, you don't want to adopt any attitudes of mediocrity.

You don't want to participate in grumbling.

Their griping.

Their goofing off.

You don't want to call in sick when you're not really sick or steal things from the supply cabinet at work when nobody's looking.

You want to be exceptional—

But without being haughty.

You must excel in everything you do.

You must demonstrate growth in your life.

In your health.

In your relationships.

In your ability to handle money.

In your community involvement.

In your speech.

In the way you treat your wife and kids.

And especially in your attitude.

In everything!

Just as my parents had a huge impact on me, shaping me into the man of God I am today, so you must be an example before you can be an effective spokesperson.

You must "show" before you can "tell."

Don't get me wrong. You don't have to be perfect. In fact, a little normalcy can go a long way. The book of James even tells us, in not so many words, that growth and change is required as we take the journey in Christ, but God doesn't condemn us because we need to grow and change. He empowers us.

He graces us.

He is our biggest encourager.

He's not expecting us to be something that we are not.

Remember, less is more!

But you do have to challenge yourself to grow in every area of your life and seek to be extraordinary in everything you do. Especially in the work you do at your assigned place of ministry—you must give more and go further than anyone else there.

You must be noticeably transformed from what you used to be.

Second, the Gospel transforms consumers into contributors.

The Corinthian believers had a lot of problems. In fact, every chapter of 1 Corinthians deals with a problem that existed in the Corinthian church.

These immature Christians were abusing the Lord's Supper. They were abusing spiritual gifts, they were highly factional, and they were looking the other way while members of their congregation committed unimaginable wrongs.

In fact, Paul's first epistle to the Corinthians was a long diatribe of correction and instruction. Perhaps this is why Paul told the Corinthians that they were acting like "mere men" (1 Corinthians 3:3, NIV).

Paul meant this as a rebuke.

We who are saved.

We who live *The Revved Life.*

We are not mere men.

We are not mere women.

We are called.

Set apart.

Made to be and do something great.

Something eternal.

The Bible makes it clear that we aren't perfect. In fact, in his letter to the Christians in Rome, Paul wrote a long explanation about his own personal struggles with sin (see Romans 7:14-25). So no Christian has ever attained the level of perfection that atheists sometimes think we should exhibit.

Nevertheless, we have been called to higher things. And we have been destined for transformation.

We are expected to be "different" and to grow every day in every area of our lives. This is especially true when it comes to our contributions to others.

Human nature is selfish. By nature, we all want things our way. And from birth, we want things our way right now.

We want our needs to be met.

We want our desires to be satisfied.

No parent ever had to teach his son to be selfish. No parent ever had to teach his daughter to be self-centered. As human beings, we come into the world with selfishness imbedded in our natures, because we have inherited natures from those who came before us.

Only Jesus can reverse this human tendency.

The change doesn't occur in a moment—but it does happen gradually over a lifetime, as we follow Christ and spend time with Him.

Because of the constant influence of God's Word and God's Spirit, we are changed "from glory to glory" (2 Corinthians 3:18, KJV). So, as we grow in our knowledge of God, we leave behind the sinful qualities of "mere men" and we increasingly take on the nature of Christ.

A little bit at a time.

SITTING WHEN YOU'RE ON FIRE

In the modern church, we have a tendency to make people new to our community "sit" for a while before we allow them to get involved in the work of the church.

We want them to "sit" under the ministry of the Word, and to "sit" under the instruction of the pastor, before they're allowed to help in the cause.

But this isn't the Biblical approach to the Christian life.

From the beginning, all Christ-followers should learn that the Christian life is about serving.

It's about giving.

And you can't really grow spiritually until you *are* actively giving and serving. In fact, the newest believers are often the most passionate servants and witnesses. So why should we make them "sit" idly on a pew, when they're so full of passion and on fire to get involved?

When you came to Christ, you were part of His problem. In fact, you were a problem for everybody.

Most people far from God create problems for their spouses.

They create problems for their families.

They create problems for their employers.

They even create problems for society as a whole.

But when a person comes to Jesus, the Lord starts to change all that.

Christ wants to make that person part of His solution: part of His solution for the church, for the community, and for those he knows and touches on a daily basis.

While such a person used to be a "consumer," devouring everything around him to satisfy his own appetites, through Christ he becomes a "contributor," constantly looking for new ways to sacrifice himself and his resources for the benefit of others.

While such a person used to deplete the time and resources of others by creating constant problems for them, through Christ he becomes a positive force, impacting others and inspiring them to turn their lives around.

To truly make an impact on the people around you, stop being a consumer.

And start being a contributor.

Stop being a complainer and a whiner and start being positive with your words. Stop being a taker and start being a giver. Stop being part of the problem and start being part of God's solution in every environment where He places you.

Make sure you leave more than you take.

Make sure you give more than you require.

Make sure you lend more than you borrow.

Be bold.

Go the extra mile.

That's how the Gospel transforms the living into the dead.

That's right! You read it correctly.

The Lord transforms the living into the dead.

Of course, the statement is correct the other way around too:

He also transforms the dead into the living.

In fact, that's how He starts the whole process of transformation. Through the faithful witness of someone who is willing to go for it, God reaches out and touches people with the Gospel. And when those people decide to believe the Gospel and to accept God's gift of eternal life, they are reborn spiritually.

In a spiritual sense, those who are dead to God are born again, and they become alive to God through Christ.

But then, God starts the lifelong process of transforming the living into the dead.

As we grow spiritually, He requires us to "die" to those things that were part of our past. He requires us to "die" to our own selfish desires.

To "die" to our insecurities and fears.

To "die" to depression.

To our old ways of thinking and behaving.

And to our false expectations of life.

The Apostle Paul explained it like this: He said, "I have been crucified with Christ" (Galatians 2:20, NIV). In other words, the old Paul was put to death, and the new Paul was resurrected through Jesus.

But Paul explained that this spiritual death was not instantaneous for him; it was a gradual, ongoing, daily thing (see 1 Corinthians 15:31). In other words, Paul was learning every day to put behind him the things that were no longer beneficial to him, now that Christ was the centerpiece of his life.

And Paul wanted all believers to do the same thing in their lives: He wanted them to learn to discard those old behaviors.

Old attitudes.

Old convictions.

Old beliefs.

Old friends.

Old enemies.

Old thoughts.

Old plans.

Old addictions.

And old obsessions that used to dominate their lives.

He wanted them to make Jesus an increasingly important part of their lives as they relegated all these lesser things to a lower status in their lives.

Daily, Paul wanted believers to "die" to those things that used to consume their time and affections, yet which have no eternal relevance or the ability to impart spiritual life.

To die, and find life.

DEAD, YET?

Are you dead yet?

Have you "died" to those things that are unproductive and unrewarding?

To those things that distract you from your real purpose in life?

From your true destiny?

Has your language changed?

Have your trash-talking days bit the dust?

Have your TV-viewing habits changed?

What about your circle of friends? Has that changed, too?

Has your attitude, your character, the way you treat children and members of the opposite sex changed?

If not, you need to get busy dying!

You need to realize that many attitudes, actions, and beliefs aren't important. They aren't giving you anything in return for your devotion. They've sucked your life dry.

You've been created for something greater.

You've been called to a higher plane of living and a higher level of expectation.

You are God's child.

The beautiful thing about the Christian life is that *you* don't have to change yourself. Just keep spending time with Jesus—He'll do the rest.

I want to remind you once again: growth and change are both required as we take the journey in Christ, but God doesn't condemn us because we need to grow and change.

Every day, He will "touch" something new in your life. He'll "touch" this attitude or that behavior. He'll "touch" this way of thinking or that bad habit in your life.

And He'll put gentle pressure on your heart, until you surrender that area of your life to Him.

Listen: If you withhold that thing from the Lord, you will feel His loving pressure increase on your heart.

But if you surrender it, He'll replace it with something better. And you will never miss what you left behind.

Because God's love *transforms*.

He is the changer of men. Women, too.

God is amazing.

The continued life change given by the Lord will impact the way you live your life. It'll speak volumes. You'll have the only kind of street cred that matters—the kind that comes from walking the walk of faith with our Savior.

And there never has been and never will be anything equal to it.

So be bold.

Be real.

Be available to the Lord.

And become a living testament to others.

An instrument in the hands of a Master Physician.

ACT 2: THE ADJUSTMENT

Breathe. Take a breath.
Let's call time out. Before we take another moment together.
Following Christ will cost.
Something.
Everything.
It's worth it.

Jesus isn't a GPS you can stick on your dashboard and expect to be guided on the easiest possible route.
NO WAY.
Giving your faith pole position in your life will often take you places you don't want to go.

YES.
Go anyway.

God didn't seek you.
Save you.
Change you.
Fill you.
Instruct you.

So that you could play it safe.
Avoid risk.
Huddle.
And hide.

That's not *The Revved Life*.

When you get to the end of this writing, I am going to ask you to start using your voice for Christ.
Ahead of everything else you talk about.
Like your cherished things.
Your iPhone.
Favorite restaurant.
Beloved store.
Even, (gasp) your political persuasion.

I think you get it.
Those living *The Revved Life* don't use their voice so they can be seen.
They reach people for a greater reason.
This is the only lesson you, as a Christ-follower, must learn.

Real Christ-followers don't use their influence for notoriety.
They don't do it for money.
Pats on the back.
Or Twitter followers.

They do it because they cannot stand people not knowing about the love of God.
About His grace.
About His justice.
The whole enchilada.

Real Christ-followers wake up daily with a person to tell.
Even if they aren't certain who that person is.

They pray.
Throwing aside every excuse.

The Revved Life knows there's no one else to do their task.
So they must.

The Revved life shows up.
Ready.
Whether their readiness is needed.
Or acknowledged.
Or important.
Showing up ready is major.

Of course there is a great contradiction to all of this.
As we walk away from pleasing people and living our faith privately.
As we use our voice and influence to reach those far from God ...
More people will listen.
In our intentions to put the focus on Christ,
And remove attention from us,
We will fashion an incredible, remarkable work.
A beautiful story.

And more people will follow.
And God will reward.
But not yet.
There's work to do.

Until then, there are no more excuses to not do what Christ commanded.
None.

PART 5

THE THEOLOGY OF *THE* *REVVED* LIFE

CHAPTER 26

THE WHY
AND WHY NOT

*I will proclaim the decree of the LORD: He said to me, "You are my Son;
today I have become your Father. Ask of me, and I will make the nations
your inheritance, the ends of the earth your possession.*

—Psalm 2:7-8, NKJV

In our world, we spend a lot of time trying to do two things:

Understand *what* people do.

And understand *why* they do it.

Marketers promoting their products, politicians searching for votes, and scientists looking for answers want to know what people tend to do.

Just as important, they want to know *why* people do the things they do.

See, to understand what drives a man to watch football games on Sunday afternoon—or what drives a woman to purchase a new pair of shoes at the mall—is to help the creator of these things understand how to capitalize on the motivations of the people they are targeting.

At this point, we've come to understand *what* the Lord wants us to do as individuals and as His church. We've seen that God wants His people to "go into all the world and preach the gospel to all creation" (Mark 16:15, NIV).

We've seen that He wants us to "go and make disciples of all nations, baptizing them in the name of the Father and of the Son and of the Holy Spirit, teaching them to obey everything I have commanded you" (Matthew 28:19-20, NIV).

We've fully analyzed the words of Jesus regarding *The Revved Life*, and we've studied the emphasis that the early church placed on *The Revved Life*.

We've explored the principles that guided the earliest believers into the uncharted waters of personal evangelism.

But the time has come for us to ask the most important, the most crucial, the most earth-shaking question we could possibly ask, regarding reaching people far from God.

The question is:

Why does the Lord want us to reach out to others in order to share His name and His plan of salvation?

This is where theology comes into play.

Now I realize that the word *theology* has a negative connotation for a lot of Christians.

I mean, usually when we think of theology, we think of Einstein-level brainiacs poring over dusty volumes of ancient books, hunting for cleverly-concealed shades of meaning in tiny little words, and written in strange languages that don't even exist anymore.

We think of boredom.

We think of microscopic tidbits of information that have no relevance in the real world.

But if this is your image of theology, you've been shown an inaccurate interpretation of this ever important topic.

Theology is simply what God has to say about a particular subject.

In fact, the word *theology* comes from two Greek words: *Theos* is the Greek word for "God," and *logos* is the Greek word for "word." So theology is simply "God's Word" on a particular subject.

If you want to know what God has to say about working, for instance, that's theology.

If you want to know what God thinks about stealing, that's theology.

If you want to know what God thinks about dating, that's theology.

Theology is simply finding everything God has to say about a particular subject, and then compiling all of His wisdom about that subject into one concise definition.

So what is God's theology about working?

He is for it.

What is God's theology about stealing?

He doesn't like it.

What's God's theology on dating?

You should, but not too early. And not without Jesus at the center of your life and relationship.

Theology, therefore, is the search for the bottom line, the search for the truth, the search for the ultimate reason we should run toward something or run away from it.

It's the search for the very clear message of God.

Now as a Christian, you undoubtedly attend church. But do you know *why* you should attend church? The answer is in the <u>Bible</u>.

As a Christian, you probably give to the work of your local church. But do you know *why* you should give? The answer is in the <u>Bible</u>.

The <u>Bible</u> speaks to most of the important issues of our lives. So to read the <u>Bible</u> and discover how God thinks about a particular issue is to "do theology."

It's that simple!

THE ALL-IMPORTANT WHY

With this definition in mind, let's ask the all-important question again.

Why should I pick up this call to reach people far from God to stick my neck out and possibly make a fool of myself, in order to tell people about Jesus Christ, my Savior?

Why?

Let's spend some time answering this question.

Let's find out what God has to say about it.

Let's build a theological basis to either support or deny the necessity for sharing God's plan of salvation with people far from Him.

And if reaching people proves to be all-important in the mind of God, then let's determine exactly *how* important it is. Where does it fall on God's scale of priorities?

There are five Biblical truths we need to consider.

CHAPTER 27

NUMBER 1: PEOPLE ARE SPIRITUALLY EMPTY

In an interview with Barbara Walters in 2001, the actor Richard Dreyfus said, "Every time I have a birthday, every time I blow out the candles, every time I see a shooting star, I wish for the same thing. I wish for inner security."

Inner security my friends is an illusion. Weeks after my mother and father crashed on Alaska Airlines 261, the *Seattle Times* came to my house to ask me about life in times like these. I made this statement, "Security is an illusion. The only secure thing about life is that everything will change."

Friends. We won't live forever. One person out of every one leaves this planet in a body bag. Change is imminent. In your life and in mine.

I am not trying to be morbid or scare you. I am trying to get you to realize that everyone is looking for security, but security is an illusion. What we need more than security is peace.

I think Richard meant *peace.*

People are spiritually empty, because they're separated from God. They know He exists, but they don't know Him personally. And they can't "see" Him or "hear" Him, because the sin in their lives is so loud it cuts them off from His presence.

The <u>Bible</u> speaks of this spiritual reality as "darkness."

People who don't realize their own spiritual origins or their own spiritual destiny are fumbling about in the darkness.

They're trying to find something to hold on to.

Trying to find something meaningful to live for.

But they can't find anything.

Everything they pour their lives into keeps coming up empty.

Everything they love lacks the power to love them in return.

Everything they pursue ends up hollow when they finally obtain it.

Everything they desire ends up worthless, and incapable of satisfying the human longing for fulfillment.

Even some of the wealthiest, the most successful, the most applauded actors and actresses in Hollywood find no inner peace in the things they've achieved in life.

People just don't know!

They just don't know that they were created by God for one primary purpose.

To fellowship with Him.

And enjoy Him forever.

They don't know that they came from God, and will return to God when they die.

They don't know that there is the principle of sin at work in their lives. Sin controls and steers every facet of their lives, and separates them from the God who made them.

And God who loves them.

They just don't know that God has a solution for this problem—and the solution is found in the death and the resurrection of Jesus Christ.

They don't know that they can be reunited with God, and that the barrier which separates them from God can be erased.

Removed.

Destroyed.

In the beginning, God created man and woman in His own likeness (see Genesis 1:26-27) and God enjoyed unhindered fellowship with man. God even met with man daily in the Garden of Eden, just to visit and talk (see Genesis 3:8). But man willfully and knowingly disobeyed God, so He was compelled to separate Himself from man.

Because God is holy, He can't look upon evil or have fellowship with unrighteousness (see Habakkuk 1:13). So man died the day God separated Himself from man, due to man's sin.

Sure, it took a while for the effects of this spiritual death to take hold of humanity. For a while, men and women continued to live for hundreds of years. But over the generations, life expectancy gradually declined.

At the same time that man's body was beginning to feel the effects of separation from its creator, man's soul was also being affected by this separation.

Violence became commonplace in the earth (see Genesis 4:23).

Pride and arrogance became commonplace, too (see Genesis 4:24; 11:4).

And man became openly defiant of the God who'd given him life; just a few generations earlier (see Genesis 6:5-6).

Since the fall of Adam and Eve in the Garden of Eden, the human race has degenerated spiritually. Of course, we've improved our plight in other ways.

For instance:

In our education, in our skills, in our understanding of how things work, we've grown and improved over time.

We've evolved mentally and culturally.

But spiritually?

Spiritually we are still separated from our Creator, the true source of life. And for this reason, our lives are empty.

Our lives are filled with comforts.

With computers and cell phones and video games.

With things.

But our lives are not filled with *life*.

Our hearts are empty, our purpose is lacking, and all of us find ourselves searching every day for the meaning of life and for the meaning of our own existence.

And to make matters worse, we add our own personal sins to the problem of sin we inherited from Adam, and separate ourselves even further from the Lord.

Or we know these things…but we don't give them credence any longer…we've lost sight of what made us …

SOMEBODY LIKE YOU

The prophet Isaiah told the Jewish people, "Your iniquities have separated you from your God; your sins have hidden His face from you, so that He will not hear" (Isaiah 59:2, NIV).

Isaiah also told the Lord, "No one calls on Your name or strives to lay hold of You; for You have hidden Your face from us and made us waste away because of our sins" (Isaiah 64:7, NIV).

As long as people don't know that God has provided a remedy for the problem of sin, they won't be able to take advantage of the free gift of eternal life God's made available to every man and woman.

They'll never realize what life can be like with the Lord.

They won't know that they can be restored to fellowship with the One who made them.

Somebody had to tell you. Right?

Somebody will have to tell *them*.

Somebody bold.

Somebody compassionate.

Somebody on fire for God.

Somebody who believes.

Somebody who still battles their own feelings of insecurity— but isn't afraid to admit it.

Somebody willing to be obedient.

To make a stand.

And do it for the glory of the One who made us.

Somebody like you and me.

CHANGED IN THE BLINK OF AN EYE

According to the Bible, people are spiritually "dead" (see Ephesians 2:1, Colossians 2:13). They don't realize that there is such a thing as spiritual life. They don't realize that it's possible to know God and to commune with God in a personal and intimate way.

They don't know that their lives can be changed in the blink of an eye and their destinies can be rewritten in an instant.

People only know what they know, until they know something else.

This is why God needs you to talk to people on His behalf. Nobody can testify for the Lord more passionately and more convincingly than someone who's truly been changed by Him.

Seriously guys, just think about it!

Have you ever discovered something wonderful in life?

A fantastic fishing hole? Wait. Bad example. I've got friends who won't tell nothing 'bout their fishing holes.

Most often the most amazing discoveries we make are shared with everyone in our lives.

An amazing phone app that went above and beyond your expectations or the advertisement's claims?

A great plumber who could fix things fast and who charged a small fee for his services?

Now ask yourself this:

How did you discover this wonderful thing?

Did somebody tell you about it? Of course! And now that you've discovered this too-good-to-be-true person or product, what are you compelled to do?

That's right! *Tell people!*

You can't wait to tell people.

You can't stop talking about it.

You can't keep it to yourself. You want to post it on Facebook, email it to your friends, or hype it big-time in your blog.

In fact, in this day and age of advanced technology, entire online corporations have been created just to help people tell other people about the good things they've discovered in life. Angie's List is a perfect example.

Well, this kind of social networking isn't new; it's actually quite old.

See, God was the author of the original social network when He compelled His followers to "go into the highways and hedges, and compel them to come in, that my house may be filled" (Luke 14:23, KJV).

God created our need to share.

God cares about the people He's made.

He loves them.

He died for them.

But these people can't receive the benefits of God's love and forgiveness. They can't be restored to Him and reconciled to Him. Unless somebody *tells them.*

It's such a heart-break when God has provided for humanity the free gift of eternal life, but nobody bothers to tell people about it.

And please don't make the excuse for yourself that people will hear the Gospel on their own. Sure, most Americans know *something* about the Gospel. They may have heard portions of it here and there. But the version they've heard has been distorted and twisted and warped by the media and by pop culture.

The political platforms are not differentiating the love of Jesus Christ from that of any other religion in the world. It's truly a shame because the real, authentic, indisputable gift of love is available to every person on the planet!

Besides, the true Gospel never grips the individual human heart until it's presented in a personal way.

You accepted Christ after you heard the Gospel in a personal way.

Others are bound to do the same.

So that's where you come in.

You are God's messenger.

You are God's ambassador.

You are God's representative.

His voice.

His hands.

His feet.

His instrument.

God put certain talents in your life, and opened certain doors of opportunity to you, because it was His will from the beginning.

He put you in a particular place of ministry where you could tell others about His love and His solution for the problems in their lives.

Regardless of how they try to hide it or cover it over with distractions, the people far from God around you are people who are spiritually empty. They need the Lord.

They require His grace.

They need His forgiveness.

They need His presence and His blessings in their lives.

They need to hear what God has in store for them—and you've been placed in "your royal position for such a time as this" (Esther 4:14, NIV).

CHAPTER 28

NUMBER 2: PEOPLE ARE LONELY

lbert Einstein said, "It is strange to be known so universally and yet be so lonely."

This awesome pearl of wisdom from one of the world's greatest thinkers accurately portrays the way many people feel.

Allow me to demonstrate.

You've probably heard of *American Idol.*

American Idol is one of the most popular TV programs of the past decade. In fact, for the past many years the show's drawn record audiences.

The premise of the show is that anybody can audition for the competition. And eventually, through a series of elimination rounds, the most talented singers in the nation are allowed to compete for the coveted title of "American Idol."

But did you know that more than *100,000 people* turn up each year to audition for this show?

Apparently, more than *100,000 people* believe they have the talent to be America's best singer!

But I think there's something more behind these numbers.

I believe the vast majority of these people just want to be celebrated.

They want to stand on a stage under the bright lights with TV cameras zooming in on them and hundreds of people watching them from the studio and millions more watching at home.

They want to hear the applause of their admirers.

They want their photographs in magazines and on the cover of a CD.

And they want hordes of screaming fans begging for an autograph while the photographers plead for them to pose and flash bulbs are popping all around them.

They believe only then they will be important or significant.

WHERE LIFE IS FOUND

People want significance.

Okay, I get that. And I understand that.

We all want to count, and I understand that, too.

But as Einstein observed, *fame* is not the same as *significance.*

Being *known* is not the same thing as being *recognized.*

Think about that.

Think about all the celebrities who fall apart, soon after achieving the notoriety, the mega-bucks, and the fame they so desperately pursued all their lives.

How many movie stars end up in prison?

How many pop culture icons end up in rehab?

How many celebrities wind up in detox?

How many rock stars and American "idols" end up in the morgue before they've lived half their lives?

The lesson we can learn from this phenomenon of Western culture is that *life isn't found in the external things.*

It isn't found in fame.

In fortune.

Or in reputation.

It isn't even found in success.

Life is found in knowing others intimately.

Including God.

And it's found in being known by others intimately.

Including God.

But what's the definition of intimacy? It's being *fully known* and *fully accepted.*

In the end, there are only three things that truly matter in life. And the older you get, the more you come to realize that your relationship with God, your relationship with the people you love, and the pursuit of your own destiny are all that really matter.

And those who have not bought into these three things, but rather into all the wrong things, have a deep sense of regret and a deep gnawing inside their souls that they've wasted their lives.

We all know people like that. Friends like that. Family like that.

Oh, they'd never say so out loud—but deep down inside they'd like to turn their ship around.

They just don't know how.

That's where you come in.

People need to know that they have a destiny in this world and for eternity.

They need to know that life consists of more than just accumulating cash and racing from one fleeting pleasure to the next.

They need to understand that life has purpose, and that God created them for purposeful living.

They also need to know that God loves them, and that He wants to have a personal, intimate relationship with each of them. He wants to get involved in their lives, and He wants to get to know them.

But God also wants each person to have a meaningful and fulfilling life with others. So God wants to develop, repair, and restore people's relationships.

He wants people to have strong marriages.

Happy homes.

He wants them to have lots of genuine friends.

He wants them to have fulfilling work.

He wants them to be respected and well liked, too.

And God wants all these earthly relationships to be right. He wants them to be free from conflict.

Free from deception.

And especially free from cruelty and abuse.

God wants to enrich our lives with a fulfilling purpose and with love. He wants us to share our lives with others, and He wants us to be able to enjoy open and mutually rewarding relationships on multiple levels.

This is one of those areas where you can easily *show* people the right way, before you *tell* them the right way.

For example:

When your wife calls you at work, or your husband visits you at the office, you can make a tremendous impact on people by the way you speak to your spouse.

You also can make a huge impact by the way you speak *about* your spouse, when he or she's not present.

The love you show gets noticed by others.

The same goes for your children and your parents.

Your pastor and your friends.

The way you treat people and the way people treat you, the way you talk about people and the way people talk about you, can say volumes about the work that Christ has done in your life and in your relationships.

FEELING LIKE DAVID

People are tired of pretending to be someone they aren't, just so they can impress those who don't really care about them anyway, or build a reputation that will become impossible to maintain.

They're tired of the divisions that exist between them and the people in their lives.

They're tired of keeping secrets, and having separate lives from the people who should be sharing life with them.

People want to be known.

They want to be accepted.

They want to be loved.

Because they are *lonely.*

Even when they're surrounded by friends and family, or hordes of adoring fans, they're lonely—because loneliness stems from a lack of intimacy.

Not from a lack of name recognition.

People are separated from others because of their inability to understand them. They're separated because of their inability to see the world through others' eyes. They're separated because they're flawed and selfish. They're separated because they've made mistakes that others can't forgive.

And for which they can't forgive themselves.

They're separated because they've been rejected in the past or because they've failed and they're embarrassed.

They feel like David when he was being hunted down and pursued by King Saul, and wrote, "My friends and companions avoid me because of my wounds; my neighbors stay far away" (Psalm 38:11, NIV).

This is why God wants people to know that He sees them, and that He cares about them.

This is why God wants to share His love and concern through the sound of your voice and the warmth of your presence.

This is why He wants you to share the good news with them—that His love is unconditional, and that He already knows their deepest feelings and deepest needs. He wants them to know that there is an amazing spiritual family waiting to adopt them, and a great company of Christ-followers who want to get to know them.

But most of all, He wants them to know that He desires to be their Father, and their closest friend.

CULTS, GANGS, AND INTIMACY

There are two groups of people whose ranks are swelling by the day.

Know who they are?

While most churches struggle to grow, cults and street gangs are springing up in record numbers.

But have you ever wondered why people would abandon the safety and security of a normal life to attach themselves to these kinds of dangerous groups?

A lot of people will enthusiastically align themselves with cults and gangs, and join them because these cults and gangs have learned to exploit the basic human need for one thing.

Intimacy.

And that's why people are flocking to join them.

Members of the hard-core gangs aren't usually upstanding citizens. Right? They're usually junkies or drug traffickers, and are often thieves and murderers.

But one thing's for sure: the members of a gang are *loyal* to one another.

They'll fight for one another and die to avenge a fellow gang member's death.

They treat one another like family, and they give each other a reason to live in a world that is otherwise empty for them.

The same is true of most cults.

Once you become a cult member in good standing, nothing on earth can separate you from the "love" of the other members. They'll stick with you through thick and thin. And people are genuinely attracted by this aspect of cult life, because this practice meets one of the deepest needs of humanity—

The need to be *known* and *accepted* by others.

These two examples are pretty extreme—they're unhealthy, exploitative, and dangerous. But it speaks to how hungry people are for love and acceptance.

That's why the church's inability to aggressively move beyond its own walls and dive in and get involved with people who need God's love has helped to bolster the membership of cults and gangs.

But the best way to counter Satan's substitutes for the church is not by opposing them with our words—but rather by simply meeting the same legitimate needs of people, the way Jesus did when He ministered to them on His earthly sojourn.

Know them.

Accept them.

Be loyal to them.

The best way to build the church and to increase the rosters of heaven is by showing people that we love them. And by informing them that God loves them.

Even the most famous, sought-after and prominent people are lonely—and they're looking for something more genuine and fulfilling to give completion to their lives.

But they'll never find answers to the loneliness if they sit silently and avoid getting involved in their lives.

And guys, it's the same for each one of us.

If you prefer your own personal space, and your own little clique of friends, more than you prefer telling others about God's love, the lonely people around you will never know how rich their lives can truly be.

They won't know their lives can change.

They won't know acceptance.

Or loyalty.

Or friendship.

They won't hear the Word.

If we don't open up our hearts and spread the Word.

CHAPTER 29

NUMBER 3: PEOPLE ARE ASHAMED AND WANT GRACE

There are many reasons for sharing the Gospel.

The Gospel has the power to impact every aspect of our lives. It can impact the feelings we hold about ourselves. It can change our relationships. It can open new doors of opportunity to us.

In fact, it can forever alter a person's destiny.

It can directly impact a person's financial wellbeing.

His attitudes and values.

Even his physical health.

The benefits of serving God are truly endless. But the primary reason for sharing the Gospel with people is to affect their eternal wellbeing.

The Bible makes it clear that "all have sinned and fall short of the glory of God" (Romans 3:23, NIV). The Bible also makes it clear that "the wages of sin is death" (Romans 6:23, NIV). People are spiritually lost and, because of the presence of unforgiven sin in their lives, they are destined to spend eternity apart from the Lord.

Deep inside, people know this is true.

People feel "dirty" inside. They feel "dead."

They feel like something is missing.

They feel guilty for the things they've done and ashamed of who they are.

And what's worse is they think they can't do anything to change these feelings and these perceptions.

So people protect themselves from these horrible thoughts, by ignoring them and refusing to think about them.

They don't want to ponder eternity, because their hearts tell them that they're accountable to their creator, and that they'll stand in judgment before Him one day.

They estimate that He will disapprove of them when that day finally arrives.

They also assume they will be condemned and they believe there is nothing they can do about this horrible predicament.

So they bury their heads in the sand, and try to pretend that it isn't real.

They ignore it, and hope it will go away.

And when they're finally forced to think about these things, at funerals and at other key moments in their lives, they just wrap the realities of death and judgment in popular fables designed to help them deflect the truth and cope with the fear.

This is why it's so painful for some people to hear about God. Jesus. The Gospel.

This is why many of them will run and hide, and do everything in their power to avoid dealing with the subject.

This also explains why some people will persecute you, taking a proactive posture in their efforts to silence your message. They'll go on the offensive, and come after you with a vengeance in order to make it clear that you should take your testimony elsewhere.

They don't want to hear the Gospel.

Not because they disbelieve it—but because they *do* believe it.

And because they don't want to *deal.*

But what they don't know is that God has a solution for this problem.

They don't know that Jesus has taken their sin upon Himself.

They don't realize that they won't be required to *earn* their way into heaven, or to make penance for all the mistakes of the past.

They don't know that salvation is a free gift of God, given to all without precondition.

They don't know that only one thing is required of them:

Simple faith.

Instead, their concept of salvation is to stop sinning and start living the perfect, ascetic lifestyle of a monk, until they can somehow appease God for all the mistakes and the screw-ups they've made in the past.

Ok, maybe not a monk. But they think faith has to do with them doing the work to change.

Or living a certain way.

They've tried to change the way they've lived before to no avail.

They've not rested in the truth that the only being who can change a human is God the Father.

They think they have to stop enjoying life, and withdraw to become hyper-spiritual and legalistically rigid. But they can't stop sinning, and they know they won't be able to live up to this preconceived notion. They know they can't be perfect.

And they know they don't want to stop laughing and living and enjoying life with those they love.

So they simply stick to their fears of eternity.

And they stick to their guilt and their shame.

And they do everything possible to avoid thinking about these things.

And until somebody breaks through the walls of protection they've built to shield themselves from God, they'll remain separated from the Lord.

And spiritually lost.

These people may never achieve their God-given purpose in life.

They'll live with the pain of their shame all their earthly days.

But worst of all, this means they'll remain separated from God for eternity, a fate that is too terrible to describe.

So someone must intervene. Someone must go to them—because they'll never come to us. These people won't respond to the brand new church sign on the highway, to your new website, or the invitation they receive in the mail.

They won't respond to your personal invitation to attend Easter Sunday services.

And they certainly won't show up to hear the special speaker this weekend.

In fact, these people don't even know anybody who goes to church regularly, because they've created their own little world far away from the church to protect themselves from the Lord and from any message about Him.

These people have become prisoners of their own fears.

What are they afraid of?

One thing.

They're afraid of God.

HIDING FROM GOD

That's why you, as God's messenger, must take the message to them.

As God's witness, you must boldly inject yourself into that person's life.

Sometimes that means being patient, until God provides an entry point. Once that happens you can gain entrance into the person's heart and life, showing him the truth about God and the truth about his own spiritual condition.

Take the story of Adam and Eve, for example

When Adam and Eve were in the Garden of Eden, they were so pure and innocent they didn't even realize they were naked. But as soon as they ate the fruit that God commanded them not to eat, something instantly changed, and they tasted the bitterness of shame for the very first time.

How do we know this? Because their first act after eating the fruit was to find a way to cover their nakedness!

And man has been hiding from God ever since.

Shame in the human heart is the first sign that something is spiritually wrong. Adam and Eve felt shame, because they disobeyed God. Because of their sin, they were cut off from the Lord. God no longer met with them in the cool of the day to talk and commune with them. In fact, God actually drove them out of the Garden He made for them.

But worst of all, Adam and Eve died.

They died spiritually.

And then they died physically.

In every possible way, their sin cut them off from their creator. But it all began with shame. And with a vain attempt to cover their shame.

So learn to look beyond the defense mechanisms that people build to keep you out of the secret places in their lives, and to keep God out of their hearts.

Sometimes their defenses will look like avoidance.

At other times, their defenses will look like persecution.

But you need to constantly remind yourself that these people know the pain, the shame, the fear, and the guilt associated with feeling and being far from God.

What they don't yet know is the answer to their dilemma.

And until someone shares with them the solution to their problem, they'll never know the answer.

This is why you, the one living *The Revved Life*, is absolutely necessary in God's plan of redemption.

CHAPTER 30

NUMBER 4: PEOPLE ARE AFRAID TO DIE

Guilt is a terrible thing to bear.

Regret is a terrible weight to carry.

Shame is a terrible scar to wear.

Fear is a terrible burden to endure.

But the worst thing about being far, far, far away from a relationship with God? It's that its effects continue *beyond this life*.

This little section of the book is the hardest for me to write. I will tell you why, there are just so many responses to this type of conversation, so many theologies. And frankly, I want to embrace a more liberal version of this theology.

But. I. Cannot.

I cannot write a theology about the necessity of reaching people far from God and not smack myself in the face with what people are really up against. It's sobering. It's not popular. But ...

It's real.

There are two great judgments that every man must endure. There's the judgment a man feels right now within his own soul. But there also is the coming judgment he must face in eternity.

Right now, people feel the judgment that comes from their own consciences.

They feel the disappointment that stems from their own failures.

They started out with such high expectations of life.

They possessed noble ambitions.

They had lofty dreams and goals.

They had high hopes for themselves—what they would accomplish in their lives and what kind of people they'd turn out to be.

But instead of becoming men and women of integrity, they became people with secrets.

Instead of building character, they built habits and addictions.

Instead of creating a legacy, they created problems for themselves.

And problems for others.

So people stand guilty in their own eyes, and they feel lonely as a result. But the problem doesn't end there. The internal judgment that a person feels would be bad enough by itself.

But the future actually looks bleaker to them than the present, because they're afraid of being judged one day by God.

THE BIG, LOVABLE, HUGGABLE TV GOD

If you watch TV or movies, you'll see the creative models humans have fabricated to help them cope with these realities.

In TV shows, for instance, people die and then become angels in heaven.

In movies, people die and then return to earth to live alongside their loved ones, in some sort of invisible realm.

In popular culture, death and the afterlife are almost always presented as a positive. All the "good guys" like Patrick Swayze in the movie *Ghost* get to go to heaven, no matter how they lived their lives on earth.

And, of course, there's no mention of Jesus Christ or the Gospel in any of these flicks.

People get to go to heaven, not because of the death and resurrection of the Son of God ...But simply because they are "good."

God is depicted as a big, lovable, huggable grandfatherly figure—like Morgan Freeman in the comedy *Bruce Almighty*—who just wants everybody on earth to snuggle up around His throne and enjoy Him forever.

No judgment!

No demands!

Just everlasting bliss for those who do the socially acceptable things in the eyes of popular culture!

To some extent, these fictitious representations of heaven in the movies are accurate. God *is* extremely loving, right? And He does want everybody to enjoy Him forever.

I see God going to such amazing lengths to communicate His love.

It's astounding.

It's scandalous.

And it's grace!

But the part pop culture always leaves out is the part about sin—that annoying *little* problem that keeps us separated from God and keeps us out of heaven.

In the real world, people near and far from God know that sin exists, and that it will become *the* issue for all of us on Judgment Day.

And most know that until their sins are dealt with, there can be no heaven and no "cuddling" with God.

But let's go back to the Garden of Eden. Remember the story about Adam and Eve? Created with total innocence, Adam and Eve didn't even realize they were naked until they sinned against God.

Then their eyes were opened.

Realizing they were naked after they ate the forbidden fruit, they became ashamed and attempted to cover their nakedness.

Shame was their first response to sin.

Fear was their second response.

Immediately after Adam and Eve covered themselves with fig leaves, they hid from God among the trees of the garden. And when God came to visit with them, Adam and Eve were nowhere to be found. So the Lord called to them, and Adam eventually answered. But when God asked Adam why he was hiding, Adam said, "I heard you in the garden, and I was afraid … so I hid" (Genesis 3:10, NIV).

Ever since then, man has been hiding from God. And apart from the gnawing guilt we feel, man's attempt to hide from God works pretty well.

Until the moment of death.

Because at death, we can't hide anymore.

Death immediately ushers us into the presence of God, where we stand before the One who created us.

The One who knows every word we have ever uttered.

The One who knows every thought we've ever entertained.

And the One who sees every deed we've ever performed.

That's when the truth of every man's life crashes in on him.

What hope does a man have?

OFF-THE-CHARTS

Even though no man has ever seen God, deep in our souls, each of us knows one thing.

God is awesome.

Each of us knows that He is indescribable.

Unimaginable.

He's off-the-charts powerful.

We also know that He is holy, and that we will fall horribly short of His expectations for us.

We stand guilty as charged in every way possible.

So what do we do? We ignore death and somehow vainly hope that it will just pass us by.

But guess what?

It won't.

And so deep inside we're afraid of what comes next.

Without God's remedy for sin, Jesus Christ, there is only fear and trembling.

Without the Gospel, there is no hope.

Can you feel the darkness of that section? I will be encouraged if you do.

Let it become a motivating force for you.

Let it stir your soul in a way that you will work and work to crack the code to reach people far from God.

In my favorite childhood movie it was Princess Leia who stated, "Help us, Obi-Wan, you're our only hope."

In many ways we are the vessel for God's love through Jesus Christ.

We are the gift of God to another.

We are His masterpiece.

His workmanship.

There's no time like right now to get going on helping people who are afraid of death find their way to freedom.

CHAPTER 31

NUMBER 5: GOD MADE A PROMISE HE INTENDS TO KEEP

ometimes, when we try to explain Biblical truths, we try to explain them from our own human perspective.

Now, don't get me wrong, people are important to God. He loved them enough to die for them.

But let's never forget, man is *not* the center of the universe.

He's not the ultimate reason for everything. God's glory is far more important. It's more important than all the interests and all the concerns of all the people on earth.

In fact, God created the world for His own glory and pleasure, not for man's benefit (see Revelation 4:11). And God will save lost humanity for His own glory, not for ours.

So for just a moment, let's switch perspectives.

Let's try to look at this thing through the Eye of God.

Let's get away from our flawed and broken human angle, and look at this *reaching people far from God* thing from God's perspective, and from the perspective of His own glory.

Let's get away from our anthropocentric (man-centered) viewpoint of salvation and let's start looking at the subject of redemption from a theocentric (God-centered) perspective.

What's in this for the Lord?

WHAT PAUL KNEW

Some scholars have referred to Psalm 2:7-8 as *the* key verses of the <u>Bible</u>. And I believe there's good reason to accept their conclusion—because these two verses were certainly the key evangelistic motivation for the early church.

The best way to understand the theology that drove the early church is to pay attention to the sermons their leaders preached when those leaders got the opportunity to share the Gospel with the masses.

Perhaps the greatest theologian in the early church was the Apostle Paul. He was certainly the only leader who achieved notoriety as a formally trained scholar in the Word of God.

According to Paul's own acknowledgement of his achievements, he was "a Hebrew of Hebrews… a Pharisee" (Philippians 3:5, NIV).

He also was "faultless" (Philippians 3:6, NIV) in matters pertaining to the Old Testament Law.

And he was personally trained and mentored by Gamaliel (see Acts 22:3), perhaps the most renowned and respected member of the Sanhedrin at that time.

So Paul was no ordinary man. He was exceptionally well educated and knowledgeable in the Word of God. In fact, because of his advanced standing among the scholars of his day, Paul was entrusted with the responsibility for leading the fight against the sect of Christians that was threatening the status quo.

Paul was admired and respected, and he held theological credentials that were beyond reproach.

He knew the Scriptures.

JESUS CHANGED

With his rich and diverse background in Old Testament theology, it's interesting to note that Paul, in his very first recorded sermon, referred back to Psalm 2:7 as the basis for his arguments.

Preaching the Gospel in the synagogue in Pisidian Antioch, Paul systematically recounted the spiritual history of Israel, in order to show the Jews and Jewish proselytes how Jesus of Nazareth fit into the history of Israel.

Then Paul boldly proclaimed the crucifixion and resurrection of Jesus, the heart of the Gospel.

But when Paul began to proclaim the resurrection of Christ, he quoted Psalm 2:7, as his Old Testament proof text:

"You are my Son; today I have become your Father."

What was Paul doing?

He was connecting Psalm 2:7 with the resurrection of Christ.

He was saying to the Jews that it was the resurrection, which proved the fact that Jesus was indeed the Son of God, and that God was indeed His Father.

In fact, it was the day of the resurrection when God *became* the Father to His Son, by openly vindicating His Son and by openly displaying His Son to the world as the risen Messiah.

So this quotation within Paul's first evangelistic sermon directly connects Psalm 2:7 with the resurrection of Jesus Christ, and undeniably establishes Psalm 2:7 as the basis for Paul's ministry.

So with this in mind, let's read the entire sentence from Psalm 2:7-8, to see what the theological implications of the resurrection would be from the perspective of the Old Testament.

Speaking prophetically on behalf of God to his Son, King David wrote, *[7]I will proclaim the Lord's decree: He said to me, "You are my son; today* (the day of the resurrection) *I have become your father. [8]Ask me, and I will make the nations your inheritance, the ends of the earth your possession.* (Parentheses mine).

So in Psalm 2:7, King David, writing on behalf of the coming Messiah, was predicting the resurrection of the Messiah.

But in Psalm 2:8, David was describing for us the aftermath of the resurrection.

God would raise His Son from the dead and display Him before the entire world as His only begotten Son.

God would vindicate Christ, and prove to the world through the resurrection that Jesus was indeed the Messiah.

And the Son of God.

But then, because of the resurrection, the Son would have the right to make a request of the Father. Because of His faithfulness in suffering, the Son would have the right to approach the Father and ask Him for a reward for His suffering and death. The Son would have the right to request the nations as His "inheritance" and the ends of the earth as His "possession."

And that's exactly what Jesus did.

Just think about it!

Before His death and resurrection, Jesus would not approach the Gentiles.

He would not approach the "nations."

Jesus kept a respectable distance from them. In fact, Jesus himself said, "I was sent only to the lost sheep of the house of Israel" (Matthew 15:24, NASB).

And when He sent His disciples out to preach, to heal, and to cast out demons, Jesus was careful to instruct them to "not go among the Gentiles or enter any town of the Samaritans. Go rather to the lost sheep of Israel" (Matthew 10:5-6, NIV).

Jesus knew that His mission on earth was limited to the house of Israel. After all, He was the Jewish Messiah.

But after the resurrection, all this changed.

His focus changed.

His parameters changed.

Why? Because through His crucifixion, He'd wrestled away from Satan the title deed to the souls of lost men, and the title deed to the nations of the earth.

The nations and the peoples of the earth became His inheritance as the risen Christ.

So immediately after the resurrection, the tone changed and Jesus' words changed. Whereas before He cautioned His disciples to limit their ministry to the house of Israel, now He was commanding them to "go ye into all the world, and preach the gospel to every creature" (Mark 16:15, KJV).

And whereas before He limited His own ministry to the Jewish people, now He was directing His followers to be His witnesses "in Jerusalem, and in all Judea and Samaria, and to the ends of the earth" (Acts 1:8, NIV).

THE SHIFT

Can you sense the shift in direction here?

Can you feel the change in tone?

There were no more restrictions.

There were no more spiritual boundaries.

By virtue of the resurrection, the nations of the earth were now the inheritance of Jesus Christ.

By virtue of His sufferings, the lost peoples of the world were now the special possession of the King of Kings.

He received God's promise that all people would now come under His jurisdiction as Lord of all earth.

That's why we sing at Christmastime: *"The kingdoms of this world have become the kingdoms of our God and of His Christ."*

That's why the great Moravian Church has its corporate mission statement written somewhere on the walls or doors of every church in their organization: "To win for the Lamb the rewards of His suffering."

It's also why the various evangelical denominations of the world have sent tens of thousands of cross-cultural missionaries around the world, to penetrate every culture and to impact "every tribe and language and people and nation" (Revelation 5:9, NIV).

The peoples of the world now belong to Christ.

The kingdoms of the world now belong to Christ.

He has purchased their redemption.

He has paid for their sins.

He's won the title deed to their souls.

He's redeemed them and wrestled them away from the tight-fisted grip of Satan. And earned the power and the authority to rightly be called "Lord."

But guess what?

Somebody has to tell them!

Somebody has to make them aware!

Somebody has to point the lost soul to his redeemer!

Somebody has to spread the truth, that Christ's love saves and cleanses us of all our sins.

The Revved Life, therefore, is about other people.

But more importantly, it's about Jesus.

It's about His suffering.

It's about His death.

His resurrection.

His glory.

His inheritance.

His forgiveness.

And a promise that His Father made to Him—a promise that the Father would reward Him at the resurrection because of His faithfulness in suffering.

God would reward His Son for humbling Himself to the point of death, and would bestow upon Him the title of "Lord."

And just think! You and I have the opportunity to be part of that!

Of fulfilling this great promise!

Because, when the final soul has been won to Christ as a reward for His suffering, the end will come and Jesus will return to establish His Kingdom in the earth.

KEEPING THE PROMISE

The Bible tells us "there is rejoicing in the presence of the angels of God over one sinner who repents" (Luke 15:10, NIV).

In heaven, the most important thing is the keeping of that promise which God made to His Son.

On earth, this also should be the most important thing, to all those who know God and serve Him.

And when you factor in all the spiritual reasons that people need the Lord, it becomes obvious that there's nothing more important in the work of God than telling lost souls about Christ, and leading lost souls to Him.

And there's nothing more rewarding, either.

In fact, God will highly reward in heaven those who have joined Him on earth in fulfilling the promise He made to His Son.

So as the people of God, let's enjoy life, and enjoy the great work we do.

Let's enjoy our families and our friends.

And let's enjoy the Lord.

But let's never forget that the *main thing* is to reach people far from God for the Lord Jesus Christ, as the reward for His sufferings.

Let's never forget that the *main thing* is to focus on the eternal things of life, more than the temporal things.

And let's never forget that the *main thing* is to keep the *main thing* the *main thing*.

PART 6

THE STRATEGY FOR LIVING *THE REVVED LIFE*

CHAPTER 32

RISING TO THE GAME CHALLENGE

The fruit of the righteous is a tree of life, and he who wins souls is wise.
—Proverbs 11:30, NKJV

So far, I've shared with you a number of stories about my experiences as the owner of a racing team.

I've also shared several personal stories about my life as a racecar driver.

What I haven't shared with you is the story of how I made the switch from owning a racecar to driving one.

And I haven't told you how I transitioned from being an observer to being a participant on the track.

As I mentioned, my passion for racing was instilled by my father at a young age, long before my Dad knew Jesus or taught me how to pray. In 2001, my racing dream was realized when a buddy from childhood contacted me and introduced me to the world of NASCAR™. After that initial "baptism" into racing, and over the next several years, new drivers—as well as crewmembers—came and went. But regardless of the changes, my team maintained its presence and produced good results on the track. The Rock Church Chevrolet took home quite a few trophies and gained a ton of respect on the Northwest circuits.

Then at the start of the 2006 season, my driver—who was also my partner—announced that he wanted to retire from the sport. He'd started racing right out of high school, but that had been quite a few years earlier. By 2006, he was married and his kids were getting older. So he decided he wanted to take some time away from the sport to be a more present father and to direct more of his attention toward his family.

I thought that was a wise choice for him at the time. Then he conveyed to me that he was really excited about the coming season, and because it would be his last, he wanted to give it everything he had, hopefully racking up a championship during his final season behind the wheel.

Even though I appreciated the advance notice and the enthusiasm for the approaching year, I found myself in a dilemma and didn't know quite what to do.

You see, over six years of racing, I'd accumulated a lot of stuff.

I had racecars.

Pit equipment.

Trailers.

Trucks.

Tools.

Fabrication supplies.

I mean I had *everything* a race team owner needed to compete on a professional level! And even though I could have sold the equipment to recoup some of my money, I really didn't want to do that.

I'd invested a lot in this venture.

And I didn't want to just walk away from it.

So I went to my partner and asked him, "What do I do with all this stuff?"

And that's when my friend said the strangest thing to me.

He said, "I think *you* can race these cars. You need to start driving."

It never dawned on me that I could just get another driver for all my equipment. Or that the driver I could get might be *me*.

On the local and regional NASCAR™ circuits, there are plenty of drivers and not that many race teams. So there's always a good driver looking to join a team.

But my first instinct was to approach the problem from an owner's perspective, and to think about my investment and all my equipment.

Well, at the time, Melinda and I had no children. I knew I had the time, the passion, and the energy to put into it, and I was certain I knew enough. After six years as a co-owner, I had the jargon down, knew all the rules, and all the behind-the-scenes stuff I needed to know to compete in the sport.

Plus, I knew all the key players, and what it took to win a professional auto race.

But let's face it: I was 36 years old. No spring chicken.

I had absolutely *no* experience behind the wheel of a racecar.

Sure, I raced motocross as a kid, but I never raced anything with four wheels. And I didn't want to make a fool of myself.

But there was another thing: I didn't want to give people an opportunity to make fun of the Lord or The Rock Church.

I didn't want to be a novelty on the racetrack.

Or a token driver who pastors one of the local churches.

If I was going to drive a racecar, I wanted to be competitive.

So in September 2006, after giving this opportunity a lot of thought and prayer, I negotiated a deal with another driver, and purchased his car from him. This gave me an opportunity to drive in the final race of the season at Evergreen Speedway.

I'll never forget the experience. We happened to have Pastor Dick Iverson at the church that weekend. He was there Saturday night for my debut, along with many of my church family. For the very first time, the members of The Rock Church watched me put on a fire suit, climb behind the wheel of the number 70 car, and drive in my first NASCAR™ race.

I had only one goal in that first race: to be a gentleman on the track. Should my slow driving create a situation where the leaders would come around and lap me, I'd be a gentleman and simply get the heck out of their way.

I'd let them pass me unchallenged while I enjoyed—and *survived*—the experience of my first race.

As it turned out, I actually passed two cars during the race, and that little triumph gave me an amazing buzz and made me feel really good about myself.

Of course, there were a lot of people who criticized me for taking this step. There were people who advised me to remain in my comfort zone and not venture into the risky world of racecar driving. In life, there will always be those people who want to discourage you from pursuing the passions of your heart—

Some because they're concerned about you—

Some because they feel threatened by your journey to personal fulfillment—

And some because they feel protective of their own interests and are fearful your passions will intrude into theirs.

So I made this important step in '06 because my partner believed in me. He thought highly enough of my skills to point me in the direction of grander achievements, and I will forever be grateful for his confidence and his encouragement.

And really, that's what this book is all about. It's about doing something with your life that transcends the expectations of the naysayers—as well as some of your own limited expectations of yourself.

It's about rising to the challenge.

Believing in yourself.

Accomplishing more with your life than even *you* thought you ever could.

If you do this, others will have no choice but to take note of your life and will then be compelled to take a closer look at their own lives.

And in that way, it's about pointing people to Christ, first through the way you live and later through the story you tell about it.

THE RISE OF THE BELIEVER

In the opening chapters of this book, I wrote about the rise of the believer to his rightful place in society.

I described in detail what it meant to *be* a witness and to *give* witness for the Lord. After I explained *what* Christians should be doing to point people to Jesus, the previous part was used to explain *why* we should tell people about the Lord.

I gave you five reasons why Christians should bear witness to the Lord through their lives and their words.

But that's not enough. I have one more point I need to make before I land this plane.

Now that you know *what* you should be doing to serve God's interests in the earth—

And now that you know *why* you should be telling people about Christ and making disciples—

It's time for you to learn *how* to do it.

It's time to learn some pointers to help you present the Gospel to people in powerful and irresistible ways.

In the next few chapters, I'll offer you some advice that'll get you pumped-up to become a powerful witness for Christ in that amazing and special place of ministry where God has placed you.

DUPLICATE YOURSELF

In the end, this is what *The Revved Life* is all about. You see, Jesus came into the world for two reasons.

First, He came to become God's sacrifice for our sins. He came to take my sins and yours upon Himself, and to sacrifice His life to pay the penalty for our sins.

But there's a second reason.

Christ came to walk among us so we could listen to His words and observe Him as He lived His life. Through His life and His words, He was doing three powerful things.

He was teaching us how to live.

He was mentoring us.

And He was seeking to duplicate Himself in the world through our lives.

But what does it mean to be Christ-like?

A person who is Christ-like *thinks* like Christ.

He *acts* like Christ.

He *talks* like Christ.

He *responds* to things the same way Christ would respond to them.

Jesus invited twelve men to follow Him everywhere He went, because He wanted these twelve men to become "like" Him. That didn't mean they had to lose their individuality or their distinctive destinies in order to be His followers. No way!

It meant that Jesus wanted these men to become the embodiment of Him in the way they viewed life, the way they responded to God, and the way they lived their lives.

And since then, every person who has come to know Jesus Christ as his Savior has been given the same invitation as the apostles were given: to "follow Me."

In fact, salvation is instantaneous. Once you're saved, you can't get any more saved. If you were saved 20 years ago, you're no more saved today than you were the day you stepped up and invited Jesus into your heart. And if you should live another 20 years, guess what? You can't become any more saved than you are right now! Salvation isn't earned; it's a free gift from God. That means it's complete when we receive it.

We cannot add to it.

We cannot increase it.

We can't expand it.

Or make it any stronger in our lives.

Salvation is once and for all. But we *can* become more like Jesus. We *can* grow in our faith and our Christian experience. We *can* change with God's help. And that's what discipleship is all about.

Discipleship means gradually and steadily learning how to live out the gift of salvation that was given to us the moment we asked Jesus into our hearts. Every day, we're supposed to die to ourselves and become a little bit more like Christ in our thinking, in our feelings, in our words, and in our actions.

If you're gradually becoming more Christ-like, then the process of *The Revved Life* is little more than convincing others to become a little more like you.

Again, this doesn't mean people start dressing like you or downloading the same music on their iPod or reading every copy of those *Left Behind* novels that you enjoy. Reaching people for Christ is all about making disciples, not clones.

The purpose of your testimony is to point people toward the same God you serve, so they can start following Him as you do.

It's a little like turning a friend on to a cool new restaurant.

Imagine there's a new restaurant in town you really like. It's human nature to tell your friend about this awesome new discovery, and invite him to join you for lunch at this wonderful place. After all, you've discovered a good thing, and you want to share that good thing with those you know.

But your friend is skeptical.

Like every other person, he has his own favorite eating places, and he doesn't see a need to try something new or to venture into strange surroundings.

So what does he do? He rejects your invitation. Repeatedly. He offers lots of excuses. Things like, "Jeff, you know, I already have my own favorite eating place."

But finally, through persistence, you persuade him to give this new restaurant a go. You suggest a specific dish for him to order. You even offer to pay for the meal, because you're anxious for him to sample what you've sampled. And as he tries the honey walnut prawns you plugged him into, he's delighted.

In fact, he starts eating lunch with you at this restaurant two or three times a week.

And he starts telling his own friends about the delicious food at this new place.

And he starts inviting *his* friends to join *him*.

This is a perfect example of how discipleship works.

You speak about the restaurant the same way you'd speak about Christ. You invite your friend to the restaurant the same way you'd invite him to church. Sure, at first your friend is just following you to the restaurant. He's just tagging along. He is *duplicating* your behavior.

Once he starts tasting the food for himself, he creates his own experience and he can find his own way back to the restaurant to eat more of that delicious food. In fact, he often *goes there without you!* Because, now he has a direct connection with the restaurant that transcends his relationship with you.

But the journey began when your friend followed you to the restaurant and let you guide him through the menu and through the placing of his order.

Yet, no matter how often your friend goes to the restaurant without you and no matter how many others he may lead there, *you* will always be a vital part of his association with the restaurant.

So you can advise him.

You can direct him.

You can get him pumped-up and point him toward culinary wonders he has never sampled before.

But at first, he will only find his way there and through the menu by following you and duplicating what you do.

People who live *The Revved Life* are more complete when they make disciples of others, or "duplicate themselves." That's really what it's all about.

It's about persuading people to follow you as you follow Christ.

It's about demonstrating to them exactly how to follow Christ so they can do it on their own.

Finally, it's about teaching these people to repeat this process with their own family and friends.

CHAPTER 33

LEAVE NO MAN BEHIND

For many years, the United States Military has embraced a philosophy that sets our soldiers, sailors, airmen, and Marines apart from the rest of the world's servicemen. That philosophy has been that no man should be left behind on the battlefield. No man should be abandoned. In fact, part of the Army Ranger Creed states, "I will never leave a fallen comrade to fall into the hands of the enemy."

This means that the Army Ranger swears an oath to put himself at risk to guarantee that no fellow Ranger is left behind, whether that Ranger is killed, wounded, or captured by the enemy.

To the Ranger, war is not about his own comfort and convenience.

War is about annihilating the enemy.

War is not about picking and choosing the battles.

War is about dealing with the challenges as they present themselves.

The oath doesn't say: "I will rescue a fallen comrade *as long as it's convenient.*"

The oath to leave no man behind guarantees the sacrifice of one's own safety and security for the greater good of rescuing a fallen warrior.

What's the parallel here?

Too many Christians want Christian life to be *easy*. If Christian leaders could just promise their followers that reaching people and living *The Revved Life* would be easy and that there'd be no embarrassment, inconvenience, discomfort, or persecution, these shallow Christians would be happy to tell others all about Jesus Christ.

But if there is any risk …

Or any difficulty …

Or any pain involved …

Man, these Christians don't want any part of it! They want all the blessings of God, but they don't want to share in the spiritual warfare that's necessary for establishing God's Kingdom.

The Bible makes it clear that many people will be left behind if you and I fail to lead them to Christ. This is a Biblical teaching that a lot of Christians don't want to hear. But the serious believer can't afford to pick and choose the words of Christ he will believe and obey.

As followers of Christ, we must be willing to deal with *all* the words of the Lord.

And we must be willing to respond to them.

After all, we'll hear these same words again at the Judgment Seat of Christ, so we might as well face them head-on and deal with them now.

Jesus made it clear that salvation is not some pie-in-the-sky teaching that's meant to make us tingle with happy feelings. Salvation is serious business.

Every man, woman, and child on this planet will eventually face God in eternity, and that person will either enter into the eternal bliss of Heaven or perish in the godless eternity of Hell. It's that simple!

It's also that profound and urgent. So the faithful follower of Christ must roll up his sleeves and be willing to get a little dirt under his nails.

He must be ready to climb in the driver's seat and grab the wheel with both hands, then fire up his faith and let the mighty power of the Lord be unleashed.

BEFORE THE GROOM'S ARRIVAL

During the final week before His crucifixion, when Jesus was persistently trying to impart to His disciples a sense of urgency and priority for their lives, the Lord shared with these twelve men a series of parables about evangelism.

One of those parables was about ten virgins (see Matthew 25:1-13).

It seems there were ten young virgin women who were attending a bride at her wedding. These young ladies were given the assignment of going out to meet the bridegroom upon his arrival at the wedding feast. So the girls took their lamps with them into the dark night. Five of the young ladies were wise enough to take some extra oil with them, while the other five were too focused on the immediate excitement to think about the future.

As the story goes, the bridegroom was running late, and the time was ticking by. So while they were waiting for the bridegroom, the girls eventually grew tired and fell asleep. And then the cry arose, "Here's the bridegroom! Come out to meet him!" (Matthew 25:6, NIV). So the young ladies awoke and began trimming their lamps so they could greet the bridegroom in the darkness. However, the girls without extra oil noticed their lamps were going out, so they asked the five girls who brought extra oil to share some. But they refused. "There may not be enough for both us and you. Instead, go to those who sell oil and buy some for yourselves" (Matthew 25:9, NIV).

"But while they were on their way to buy the oil, the bridegroom arrived. The virgins who were ready went in with him to the wedding banquet. And the door was shut." (Matthew 25:10, NIV). Then later, the five unprepared virgins returned to find the door closed. They were locked out! And they were not allowed to enter or to participate in the banquet.

Jesus told this parable because He wanted His followers to know that salvation is serious business. God's not fooling around. When the end of this life comes for each of us, there won't be "second chances" to be saved.

Those who are prepared to meet the Lord will be allowed to participate in the glorious marriage supper of the Lamb.

But those who are unprepared won't be given additional time to get right with God. And no person will be allowed to "borrow" salvation from another. Each person will be required to bring his own "oil" to the feast. It's vital, therefore, that we awaken people to this reality now, in advance of the groom's arrival.

It's vital that we tell people about the Lord and make them ready for that inevitable day.

It'll be too late to share the oil of the Holy Spirit with them after we've entered the presence of the Lord and after the door is closed.

Since becoming a lead pastor, one of the things I've noticed about Christians is that too many of them are more interested in gaining knowledge than they are in sharing Christ.

Wait, time out—don't get me wrong! It's always a good thing to grow in wisdom and in the knowledge of the Lord.

And the best way to grow spiritually is to feed incessantly on the Word of God.

But while "food" is always a good thing, too much food and too little exercise can be a pretty deadly combination. To maintain physical health, a person needs to eat and then exert himself through work or exercise in order to burn up the food he's consumed.

It's the same with spiritual health: a person needs to feast on the Word of God and upon the worship and fellowship that bring strength to the bones and joy to the heart. But a person also needs to balance all this "food" with some spiritual exercise.

A person needs to get involved in the work of God's Kingdom.

And he needs to exert himself through the spiritual exercise of evangelism and reaching people far from God so he won't become spiritually fat and lazy.

Unfortunately, a lot of the Christians are people who "eat" frequently (Bible study, church attendance, fellowship), but get little spiritual exercise (ministry, serving, witnessing). Because of that, they're out of shape and spiritually unhealthy.

They're flabby Christians, because they don't do the work.

In the New Testament, winning people to Jesus is always depicted as work: "Ask the Lord of the harvest, therefore, to send out workers into His harvest field" (Matthew 9:38, NIV). We will be allowed to "rest" at a later time. "As long as it is day, we must do the works of Him who sent me. Night is coming, when no one can work" (John 9:4). But right now, we're expected to work in the fields and gather the harvest, because time is running out for these things.

The insinuation is that much work will be left undone unless we bear down and resolve to make reaching people a matter of utmost urgency.

So read your Bibles, dive into the Word of God on your smart-phone, listen to your CDs, and attend every church service and Christian conference you possibly can. But do *not* neglect going beyond those things to reach people along the way.

How do you do that?

Do what Jesus did—and intentionally venture out of your comfort zone to engage some of those people who don't know the Lord.

If you had a son or a daughter who was lost in the mountains, and nightfall was approaching, how urgently would you seek that child? Pretty urgently, right?

If you were a Navy SEAL in battle and your best buddy was missing in action, how urgently would you hunt to keep him from falling into the hands of the enemy?

Whenever a crisis hits, we naturally set all other interests aside, in order to focus on the urgent need at hand. And that's exactly what God wants us to do regarding lost souls.

According to Dr. Nick Henry, a friend of mine who conducted research for a huge foreign missionary organization, one person dies every second of every minute of every day (3,600 seconds per hour; 86,400 seconds per day) who has never heard a presentation of the Gospel.

And even though most of these people are beyond your personal reach or mine, *some* of them are within your sphere of influence.

In fact, for some of these "unreached" people, *you* are the only source of spiritual truth they will ever have in their lives!

So let a sense of urgency grip you.

Make sure no person within your sphere of influence is neglected or forgotten.

Pray for your friends, your family members, your coworkers, and everyone else who is part of your daily life.

And ask God to help you find an opening to approach these people with the Gospel.

You won't convince all of them to accept Christ. And you may not get the opportunity to speak to each of them before death claims them or Christ returns. You mustn't feel badly about that.

The clear impression in Jesus' parable about the workers in His field is that the close of the day will still leave much work unaccomplished.

And that's why it's essential for all of us to stop wasting time.

And to start making His priority *our* priority.

CHAPTER 34

NO TIME LIKE NOW

The Bible and life itself teach us that no man can predict the day or the hour when he will be called upon to present himself before the Lord.

No man can predict the day or the hour when Christ will return or when death will unexpectedly inject its bitter sting.

A couple of years ago, I received a message on my Facebook page, a powerful story from one of my church members that drives home this truth in an unforgettable way. The woman writing the message said:

"I was at a Dave Ramsey Financial Peace University seminar on Friday. There were people from all different churches there. I met a woman and she asked where I went to church. I told her I went to The Rock Church in Monroe. She started crying.

"I asked what was wrong, and she said her brother was a soldier, and one of his friends had invited him to a baptism service at The Rock Church and he went one time and brought her along. It was the only time he had been to church in his life.

"You guys did an altar call at the end of the service. She was there next to him and got to hear him pray the prayer of salvation with more gusto in his voice than she had ever heard before. The next week he was shipped out to Afghanistan and killed in action. But thanks to The Rock Church, she knew her brother was with Jesus."

The woman writing this message went on to encourage me to keep up my efforts. She encouraged me to continue giving altar calls and to continue teaching people to be witnesses in their private lives.

She went on to reiterate the importance and the urgency of telling people about the Lord and emphasizing the primary role that connecting with people who have no relationship with Jesus should play in the life of every believer.

I think this story drives home another important point.

I think it powerfully demonstrates the importance of seizing the moment.

God gives us very few moments in life where we can truly make an impact and turn things around for ourselves or other people. If we fail to make use of these opportunities, we'll stand before God one day with a painful inability to explain why we didn't take advantage of the open doors He presented to us.

This soldier, who died on the battlefield, is now with the Lord. But he's there because the people in his life took their obligation seriously to seize the moment and redeem the time.

Somebody invited this young man to church on that pivotal Sunday morning.

Somebody came along with him, making it easier for him to accept the invitation.

Somebody presented the Gospel and gave him an opportunity to respond.

And somebody respectfully and patiently waited for him as he took the time to pray.

Young people sometimes fail to appreciate the value of time, because they're so excited about the future. But the older you get, the more you learn to appreciate the preciousness of time and the importance of squeezing the life out of every day and every opportunity.

As you grow older, you remember when your children were young, and you regret the special moments you failed to embrace.

You remember the little house or the small town you couldn't wait to leave, and you start missing the people and places you used to take for granted.

You start recalling your first bicycle.

Your first job.

Your first boyfriend.

Your first girlfriend.

Your first car.

Fond memories, mixed with strange longings, begin to consume your thoughts.

Time has a way of teaching us to value time.

Time has a way of teaching us that we can't go back.

We don't all have a time-traveling DeLorean or a wormhole to zoom us back in time and undo our bad choices.

We can't reclaim the missed opportunities or the moments we took for granted.

So the time is now—right now, my friend.

Right *now* is the time to deal with those lingering struggles you've been promising God you would surgically remove from your life.

Now is the time to love your wife or your husband.

To create memories with your children.

To attend church.

To start tithing and saving for the future. And to get involved in the mighty work of the Lord.

Now is the time to get out of debt.

To break that nasty habit you've been clinging to for years.

To start doing something *meaningful* to make your lifelong dreams come true.

But most of all …

Now is the time to take action and engage people about their souls and their readiness for eternity.

Time won't wait for you; it marches on. And the only thing worse than watching time disappear over the horizon is the gnawing sense of regret we feel for failing to take advantage of it.

So get it in gear, put the pedal to the metal, and do something *today* to start turning this ship around.

Do something to act upon the clear messages that God gives you regarding your life and your purpose.

Don't just sit idly by.

Don't watch time go by.

Don't!

The person who understands the sanctity of time and the urgency of the Great Commission is the person who'll live his life every minute of every day as if the plane were going down.

He lives with the knowledge that time is fleeting.

And tomorrow offers no guarantees. In the work of God, more than any other endeavor, time is of the essence. We can't afford to squander time.

KEEP YOUR EYE ON THE BALL

The Word of God was crafted by the Holy Spirit to teach us those things we need to know in order to be saved and to fulfill God's purposes in the earth. And the Holy Spirit has chosen to give us this information in two different ways.

First, He *explicitly* teaches us God's thoughts and God's ways. In other words, He comes right out and tells us through the written Word what we should do and what we shouldn't do. "Thou shalt not steal" (Exodus 20:15, KJV) is a great illustration. "Be ye kind one to another" (Ephesians 4:32, KJV) is another.

But most of God's wisdom is not communicated through direct, explicit teaching. Most of God's wisdom is given to us through *implicit* instruction.

In other words, the Holy Spirit communicates God's wisdom without coming right out and saying it directly. Instead, He teaches us God's wisdom in a roundabout way.

Through stories.

Illustrations.

Parables.

And the eyewitness accounts of historical events.

For instance, we learn that adultery is wrong and that sexual infidelity is destructive by reading the story of David and Bathsheba. Nowhere in that lengthy narrative will you find any explicit word from God that says, "Adultery is sinful and damaging." But you still get the point by reading the story.

You see the results of adultery. You witness the consequences.

This implicit method of instruction is also the way the Holy Spirit has chosen to teach us much of what we know about *The Revved Life.*

By reading the book of Acts, for example, we see what the early believers did and we see the outcome of their actions. So, through the implications we derive from reading Acts, coupled with the explicit teachings of Scripture, we learn to look at the concept of leading people to Christ through the eyes of God.

We learn to see lost humanity from God's perspective.

And we learn about the things we must do to respond to the spiritual condition of those around us.

Now let me warn you that you should be careful when formulating your theology from the implied teachings of Scripture (the stories) rather than the explicit teachings of Scripture (the commands). Not every story in the Bible describes an act you want to duplicate in your own life.

Sometimes, we can learn what God wants us to do in our daily lives by reading about the positive outcomes of the acts of those who preceded us, and then duplicating the choices and behaviors of those who walked closely with God.

But at other times, we learn what God wants us to avoid by reading about the tragic results of the actions of people who made poor choices—and then doing everything possible to prevent a repeat of those terrible consequences in our own lives.

In fact, nobody in the Bible made more mistakes than the Jews who wandered in the wilderness for 40 years! And the apostle Paul explains, "These things happened to them as examples and were written down as warnings for us" (1 Corinthians 10:11, NIV).

But even in the midst of all the examples of sin and rebellion that we find in Exodus, Leviticus, Numbers, and Deuteronomy, the Bible gives us tons of stories about people who lived righteous lives at that time—people like Joshua and Caleb.

Bezalel and Oholiab.

Eleazar and Ithamar.

So while some of the people did great things that you and I should emulate in our lives today, others did reprehensible things.

The book of Acts is one of the all-time greatest resources for *The Revved Life*. You won't find a lot of direct, explicit teaching about *The Revved Life* in there, but what you will find are a lot of examples of people who lived winning lives, who impacted others, and changed the course of human history.

You can learn how to deal with persecution by reading about Peter and John and their encounters with the Jewish elders.

You can learn how to explain the Gospel by reading the eloquent sermons of Paul.

You can learn how to be bold and selfless in your own walk by studying the habits of the early members of the church and paying close attention to their selflessness and fearlessness.

But this doesn't mean that everything they did was perfect or something we should emulate in our lives today. Sometimes the early Christians made mistakes, just like modern Christians make mistakes.

Consequently, one of the places where the early church really messed up was in the area of focus. They took their eyes off the ball, and God had to shake them up and sort of slap them around and bring them back into focus.

You didn't realize that the early church made mistakes? Of course they did! They were human!

Sometimes we forget this when we read the Bible. We tend to look at the great men and women of the Bible as role models. And, in a sense, they should be. They were great people, and God did great things through them.

But were they *perfect?* Nope! So we must be careful when we follow their lead.

More often than not, the characters of the Bible were simple men and women just like you and me. They were everyday people who struggled with sin and who often stumbled upon the will of God by accident or by grace.

Abraham had faith that truly impressed God, but he was also a coward and a deceptive human being.

Jacob? He was the patriarch of the nation of Israel, but he was also a liar.

David was a man after God's own heart and the most notable ancestor of the Jewish Messiah, but he was also an adulterer and a murderer.

If you and I were to read the stories of these people and then gullibly follow their lead in *everything* they did, we'd often find ourselves living in opposition to God.

There is no perfect person in the Bible.

Except for Jesus.

So be careful what you take from these people's lives. Take the good parts, but reject the bad parts. This is true throughout the Bible, because even though Peter, James, John, and Paul were awesome people, they definitely had their inconsistencies and their failures, just like you and me.

So emulate their passion.

And imitate their zeal.

Respect their success.

And submit to their wisdom.

But also learn from their mistakes.

Seek to do better with your own life.

In this way, the Lord will be glorified even through the past mistakes of those who followed Him. And the will of God will be accomplished in the earth even through the failures of those who preceded us in the faith.

Isn't that amazing?

CHAPTER 35

UNFATAL MISTAKES

S
o where are these "mistakes" that were made by the early church fathers?

Well, one of them was their outright refusal to obey the last command of their Lord.

The last time He ever saw them, Jesus told His disciples to "be witnesses unto Me both in Jerusalem, and in all Judea, and in Samaria, and unto the uttermost part of the earth" (Acts 1:8, KJV).

We can learn a lot from the disciples' bold efforts to saturate Jerusalem with the Gospel. We should absolutely stand in awe of their willingness to surrender their possessions in favor of unity and their lives in allegiance to the Gospel.

But they *never* obeyed the Lord's command to go into Samaria and Judea and the rest of the world! They stayed put in Jerusalem!

And they stayed and they stayed and they stayed!

Nobody knows the exact timeline, so nobody knows precisely how long Peter, John, and the rest of the believers remained in Jerusalem before they finally left the city. But two things we know for sure.

First, we know that a great deal of time elapsed. And we're not talking about a few days or a few weeks here, folks; we're talking about *years*.

Once the Holy Spirit fell upon the early believers on the Day of Pentecost and revival broke out in Jerusalem, the disciples didn't want to leave Jerusalem. They wanted to stay put. After all, who wants to leave a place where miracles are occurring in the streets and where thousands of people are being saved in a tremendous move of God?

So the early church leaders dug in.

They set up meeting places.

They set up systems for sharing possessions and for feeding the widows.

They set up a hierarchy of leadership and authority.

They started building a structure of church authority and church ministry to help maintain the revival that was occurring in their city.

And that's an awesome thing. The results speak for themselves.

People were saved.

People were healed.

Thousands upon thousands of people had an opportunity to hear the Gospel.

But here's the problem: They weren't doing what Jesus told them to do!

Jesus told them to return to Jerusalem and to wait there "until" they received power from on high. Then He wanted them to *leave* Jerusalem in order to venture out to the other communities and nations. Millions of others needed the Gospel, too.

The members of the Jerusalem church were faithful to share the Gospel. I suppose I can't fault them for their lack of obedience. They'd seen Jesus put on a killer show, and they seized every opportunity to tell people about the Lord.

But it's equally clear that they enjoyed the familiarity of Jerusalem and the familiarity of one another's company.

They enjoyed the awesome revival that was taking place around them.

They enjoyed the excitement and the wonder of being part of such a large and growing movement.

Like I said, I can't blame them for that. There isn't anything I'd like more than to experience continual revival in my own life and in my own church. And, if a great revival broke out in Monroe, I wouldn't want to leave here either.

But the fact remains that God wanted them to go elsewhere, and they refused to go.

They said, *No way.*

They took their eyes off the ball.

So God stepped in.

He allowed a terrible persecution to rain down on the church in Jerusalem, driving them against their will into the surrounding regions.

FLIPPED

Have you ever been physically flipped upside down? It's a pretty jarring experience when you're not expecting it. I bet once you regained your bearings, you learned not to let that happen again and stay right side up.

In the same way, I'm sure life has turned you upside down and taught you something crucial you needed to know.

In similar fashion, God turned the early church upside down to get them right side up.

He took the command of Acts 1:8 and turned that command upside down in Acts 8:1 to show the church where they were going wrong.

In Acts 1:8 God gave the church its marching orders. He told them to "be my witnesses … in all Judea and Samaria, and to the ends of the earth." But when the church lost its focus and failed to do all that God commanded them to do, He took control in Acts 8:1.

In that verse, we're told: "a great persecution broke out against the church in Jerusalem, and all except the apostles were scattered throughout Judea and Samaria."

So God did not *cause* the persecution. The persecution simply "broke out."

It was the natural consequence of the light of God coming into conflict with the powers of death and darkness.

But God seized the opportunity to "scatter" the church throughout Judea and Samaria so they could do what He commanded them to do in the first place.

They had been faithful in Jerusalem. In fact, in Jerusalem the early believers were more than faithful.

They were imprisoned.

Beaten.

Tortured.

And killed because of the Gospel.

But they hadn't taken the Gospel outside the city to the rest of the world. So God allowed the cruel circumstances of life to rain down on them and influence them to do what they should have done in the first place.

This brings me to my basic point:

God made a promise to His Son that He would give Him all the people of the world as His inheritance and the nations of the earth as His possession.

And God takes this promise very seriously. In fact, the keeping of this promise is the most important priority in Heaven.

Likewise, the keeping of this promise must also be the most important priority in the church. So the church must remain focused. And the individual believer must, too. If we don't, God will certainly step in. He will intervene.

Because, He isn't playing around.

He is more than serious about saturating the world with the name of His Son.

So while there are many worthwhile and noble things a church can do, none of these transcends the primacy of reaching people far from God.

And while there are many worthwhile and noble things an individual believer can do, none of these rises to the level of being a witness of all that they've seen and heard Jesus do.

So keep your eye on the ball.

Work hard to keep the main thing in your life the main thing.

Don't let the distractions of this world deter you from your primary mission.

And don't let the urgency of other matters distract you from maintaining your passion for souls.

It's your job, as a steward of all God has entrusted to your care, to be responsible with the opportunities and challenges He has placed in your hands while keeping your witness at the forefront of your agenda.

So while you work hard to be a good husband or a good wife, a good parent or a good son or daughter, a good pastor or a good racecar driver, never get so distracted with the weight of your responsibilities that you forget to represent Christ along the way.

After all, a million years from now, most of the things that consume your time and energy at this moment won't matter.

But a million years from now, today's efforts to represent Jesus Christ will still be a life-giving tree.

And it will be bearing fruit.

OVERCOME YOUR FEARS

There's a period of time, just before a NASCAR™ race kicks off, when the speedway officials are making announcements and introducing the drivers. This can be an especially tense time for the drivers, because we know the race is about to begin. By now all the preparations have been completed, the drivers are ready, and there's nothing to do except wait for the race to begin. So your thoughts begin wandering toward those things that lie buried deep inside.

Some drivers take this time to worry themselves into a frenzy.

Some get nervous, wondering how they'll perform in the heat of competition.

Some overload on anxiety while they impatiently wait for the pace car to guide them around the track.

But like most of my fellow drivers, I take this time to make some last-minute adjustments to my car.

I check my harnesses to make sure my belts are tight.

I check my radio to make sure I can hear my spotter.

I check my window net to make sure it's secure.

And I use this time to reflect.

I think about my wife.

I think about my daughter.

I think about my family, my friends, and my church.

I think about representing all of them in a way that would bring them honor.

And then I do one last thing:

I pray.

I ask God for safety on the racetrack. I ask God to help me conduct myself in a way that will enable me to reach people on His behalf. I ask the Lord that, no matter what might happen on the track, He would help me behave in a Christ-like manner. And I ask the Lord for success. I ask him to let me be part of the show. Even if I can't win every time, I want to be competitive. I want to be up there at the front, racing for the checkered flag and the trophy.

Lots of people ask me, "Jeff, are you ever afraid before a race?"

"No, not really," I tell them. I mean, I am reflective, for sure. But I wouldn't say that I'm afraid. These cars are rock-solid machines and very safe. So I don't really deal with fear prior to a race.

Don't get me wrong. I realize that stock car racing isn't child's play. We're racing 550-horsepower, high-octane vehicles at speeds nearing 140 miles-an-hour. I have deep respect for the power of the automobile I'm driving and the speed I'm traveling.

I have a deep respect for the emotions that can flare up on a racetrack. But I don't really become fearful. Sure, I've crashed hard a couple of times, even to the point of totaling the car, being concussed, and injuring my spine.

So while I don't feel afraid as I start a race, I do have a sense of reverence regarding the nature of what I'm about to do.

And, in a similar way, you should have a reverence for what you're about to do every time you leave your home to take the Gospel with you into the workplace and into the world.

You shouldn't be afraid. But you should be aware that this isn't child's play.

You need God's direction.

God's help.

God's power.

Fear is undoubtedly the greatest deterrent to sharing the Gospel with others. Christian people are afraid of being rejected. Of being mocked or scorned. They're afraid of looking ridiculous or foolish and of being confronted with questions they can't answer.

They're afraid of being labeled a kook or a fanatic.

Fear is an absolute killer to sharing the Gospel.

And fear is definitely the primary impediment to effectively living *The Revved Life.*

In fact, *Christianity Today* conducted a survey a few years ago identifying the main reasons Christians fail to share the Gospel.

Know what the top three reasons were?

(1) Christians feel they wouldn't be able to share the Gospel with the same effectiveness as a professional minister.

(2) They're too timid and lack confidence in their abilities.

(3) They're afraid of how people might respond to them.

So ask yourself this question:

Are you afraid before your race begins?

Are you afraid when that moment arrives to start your engine and engage the others in your circle of influence? Are you afraid to make a move? Are you afraid to reach for the prize?

If so, my advice to you is this: Learn to overcome your fears. That's what I had to do. I had to stare my fears right in the face.

I race door-to-door with other drivers without any fear because I've taught myself to face my fears head-on.

By tasting some success on the track, I've taught myself to stop focusing on the wall and the other drivers.

What do I focus on?

The finish line.

But that change of perspective took time. It wasn't there the first time I climbed behind the wheel and competed in a race.

In the opening paragraphs of this section, I shared with you the story of how I made the transition from being an owner to being a driver. But I bet you figured out that I didn't win my first race. In fact, I only passed two other drivers during the entire race—one while he was spinning out of control.

But the moment I passed my first racecar on the open track became a major turning point in my life.

All I managed to do during my first race was to win one little head-to-head battle with one other driver. *That's all!*

Yet, that singular moment of triumph made me feel so good about myself that it changed me forever.

In fact, that seemingly unimportant moment of personal victory made me feel like I had just won the Daytona 500.

It built confidence in my heart.

It put a taste in my mouth for more victories.

For greater victories.

So by the time the next racing season rolled around, I was ready. I was stoked, pumped-up, prepared to run hard and compete hard.

I wasn't afraid anymore.

Nothing creates an appetite for success like success. Since the day I passed my first car in 2006, I've been unwilling to accept second place in any race.

I want to win.

And every time I win, I want to win again.

That's precisely the way it is with reaching people far from God. The best way to overcome your fear of sharing Christ with others is to share Christ with others, so you can "taste" what it's like to lead an unbelieving soul to the Lord.

Some things just can't be appreciated until you taste them for yourself. This is why the Bible tells us to "taste and see that the LORD is good" (Psalm 34:8, NIV).

For example: I love chocolate cake, but if I used the rest of the pages of this book to describe to you the sweetness and creaminess of chocolate cake, and how it melts on my tongue, you still couldn't appreciate it or develop an appetite for it until you tasted it for yourself.

But with that first bite—BOOM!—you'd fall in love with it, too.

The same rule applies in the spiritual realm.

No one can fully understand the Lord until he's "tasted" Christ himself. You can tell a person about God's goodness all day long and you can talk about the things God has done in your life until you collapse from physical exhaustion. But until a person invites Jesus into his own heart and starts relating to the Lord directly on a daily basis, that person will never understand the Lord or what it means to be a Christian.

Some things simply have to be "tasted" to be appreciated.

But once you taste them, they become an object of desire.

And so it is with *The Revved Life*.

Until you live it, you just don't know what you don't know.

In this book and from my church pulpit, I can expound all the virtues of reaching people, the importance of getting out there and doing it, and the methods of using your witness effectively in our world. But until someone actually partners with Jesus and wins a soul to Christ, that person will never know how it feels.

So if you've never personally led a soul to Christ, the best I can do to describe it to you is to say that, next to salvation, it's the greatest and most life-changing experience possible.

It's awesome.

It's amazing.

And it's addictive.

Once you win a soul to the Lord, you won't stop telling people about Christ. In fact, you'll have to learn to control yourself so you don't go overboard.

Remember, less is more and more is less.

The best antidote for fear is simply to do it.

Remember the first time you jumped off the diving board or the first time you asked a girl out on a date? Weren't you terrified? But you did it anyway. You realized that you had to do it and that your first leap was a necessary rite of passage. So you pretended to be brave and you took the plunge.

And guess what?

You didn't die.

You survived to do it again.

And over time, it actually became something you enjoyed and looked forward to.

It's a matter of getting behind the wheel.

Starting the engine.

Hitting the gas.

And running the race.

It's a matter of doing what Jesus told us to do. The fear is natural. You're normal if you're afraid.

But you can't let your fear defeat you or keep you from obeying the commands of God. If you face your fears head-on, they will have no choice but to flee from you.

You'll then have nothing standing in the way of living the fullness of *The Revved Life*.

CHAPTER 36

EQUIPPED FOR THE TASK

One of the reasons I'm not afraid when I start a race is because I'm equipped. In fact, as I explained to you in the story above, I spend the final moments just before the race checking all the equipment on my racecar. I check everything that's within my sight and within my reach, because I can never rise above the performance of my equipment. If my racecar is deficient in any way, even a perfect performance on the track will fail to lead me to victory.

This is why my crew spends endless hours building and tweaking my car, and this is why I spend endless hours testing it before I enter it in a race.

In racing, the car is key.

A perfect driver and a perfect crew are merely "average" if the car is average. They can do everything right from start to finish, but if the car isn't right, it doesn't matter.

However, a great racecar can make up for inexperience and even human error.

The car and its preparation have the capacity to determine the outcome of the race more often than the guy behind the wheel. You can't consistently win in racing unless you have a car that outperforms the other cars on the track.

So before you jump off the diving board or pop the question to a lost soul, make sure you're equipped for success.

No pro football player would ever take the field without a helmet and pads.

No golfer would ever tee off at the Masters without a set of golf clubs that were uniquely designed for him.

To skimp on equipment is to invite disaster and to spread the welcome mat for failure. But to enter the race with the right equipment is to give oneself the best chance for success.

This is true in athletics.

This is true in business.

And this is absolutely true in winning people to the Lord.

There are three pieces of "equipment" you must have before going into battle.

You need a heart of compassion.

A basic grasp of Scripture.

And you'll need "GUTS"—which I'll explain later.

As far as compassion is concerned, this is a total no-brainer.

To reach people, you have to *care* about people.

You have to care about their condition.

And you have to care that they know Jesus Christ.

Seriously, why would I want to leave the comfort of my office chair and insert myself into a coworker's life unless I cared about that coworker? Why would I want to risk rejection and ridicule within my social circle unless there was a compelling reason to take such a risk?

If I were to purchase a brand new $1000 suit, I wouldn't want to ruin that new suit by dunking it in water. But if someone I cared about were to slip and fall into a swimming pool, I wouldn't hesitate to jump in and save them, even if it meant I had to ruin my new suit.

I'd sacrifice the suit in order to save a human life, because my concern for the person's life would override my comfort, my convenience, and the value of my material possessions.

Similarly, the only force that can truly compel me to take the risks associated with following Christ is the force of compassion.

If my heart is genuinely full of love for those who are lost, I will accept the risks associated with one-on-one witnessing.

I will pay the price.

I will make the effort.

I will inconvenience myself for the sake of the person who needs the Lord.

Compassion will help you remember that lost people are truly *lost*. They are lost for eternity—but they also are lost for now. They have no bearing in their lives. They have no anchor. They have no spiritual compass. They are drifting through life like a cork on the open seas, driven unconsciously by the winds of change and the currents of popular culture.

They don't recognize their own origins as people created in the image of God.

They don't understand their own destiny as people of great purpose. So they're hurting.

They're hurting in their relationships, hurting in their hearts, and lacking in simple self-esteem. The Christ-follower must be equipped with a heart of compassion, because compassion is the ingredient that will drive him to confront the lost.

In addition to compassion, the successful witness for Christ needs a basic command of the Scriptures. Don't worry—this doesn't mean he has to be a full-blown theologian. Actually, taking a theological approach could be an impediment, because most theologians make the Bible too hard to understand.

Nevertheless, the effective witness needs to know *something* about the Bible. They need to know God's plan of salvation and need to understand the foundational teachings of God's Word. They need to be able to respond to simple questions or simple objections.

Maybe the best example of one-on-one witnessing in the Bible is the example of Philip leading the Ethiopian eunuch to Christ in

Acts 8:26-40. God directed Philip to "go south to the road—the desert road—that goes down from Jerusalem to Gaza" (Acts 8:26, NIV). So Philip obeyed the Lord, "and on his way he met an Ethiopian eunuch, an important official in charge of all the treasury of Candace, queen of the Ethiopians" (Acts 8:27, NIV).

The Ethiopian was riding along in his chariot, reading the Scriptures. And as Philip drew closer, he realized that the Ethiopian was reading from the book of Isaiah. But when the Ethiopian told Philip he didn't understand the things he was reading, Philip seized this awesome opportunity to sit down with him and explain the prophecies of Isaiah. This led to the Ethiopian's conversion and to his baptism.

Philip was equipped and ready to respond to the opportunity God presented him to lead this man to Christ.

At the end of this part, I'll offer you a simple way to present the plan of salvation, and I'll arm you with some supporting verses that you can use to explain the Gospel and to respond to people's typical objections. For now, I just want you to be aware that you cannot successfully win people without a compassionate heart and without a basic knowledge of the key scriptures.

But there is one more thing you'll need in order to be a successful soul winner.

Remember what the third thing was I mentioned?

Not only will you need compassion and a basic grasp of Scriptures, but you will also need "GUTS" ("Giving Up The Stuff") that holds you back.

In Psalm 51, we find what is undoubtedly the most heartfelt prayer of repentance in the entire Bible.

David had committed adultery, and had the husband of his lover killed in a desperate attempt to conceal his indiscretion. But through the prophet Nathan, God exposed David's sin, and now David was praying for God's mercy and forgiveness.

The prayer is passionate, and it's persuasive. It's an anointed prayer that expresses true sorrow and deep personal repentance. David doesn't hold back. He not only tells God what he's done—he also tells God what his sin has cost him. Then he pleads for God's mercy.

Then David concludes his prayer by begging God to restore him. He doesn't just want his sin erased; David *wants his life back.*

He wants his relationship with God reinstated.

He wants joy again.

And he wants the presence and the power of the Holy Spirit to consume his life once more.

So David prays, "Restore to me the joy of Your salvation and grant me a willing spirit, to sustain me" (Psalm 51:12, NIV). But then David offers an explanation for his request. It's not that he simply wants to feel good about himself again. It's not that he simply wants the burden of guilt removed from his life. It's not that he just wants his prestige reinstated or that he wants to return to his normal routines without a perpetual sense of shame.

David prays for God to *make things right in his life* so he can once again have a platform from which to tell people about the Lord.

David prayed: Do these things for me—forgive me, cleanse me, restore me—"then I will teach transgressors Your ways, and sinners will turn back to You" (Psalm 51:13, NIV). "Save me from bloodguilt, O God, the God who saves me, and my tongue will sing of Your righteousness" (Psalm 51:14). "O Lord, open my lips, Lord, and my mouth will declare Your praise" (Psalm 51:15, NIV).

David wanted to testify.

He wanted God to make things right in his life and to restore him, so he could "unbutton" his lips and start telling people once again about the faithfulness and power and majesty of the Lord.

David wanted to sing once more about the Lord. He wanted to write songs again.

He wanted to declare God's praises again.

But David couldn't do these things until he removed some "stuff" from his life and made some things right with the Lord. He had to give up some things that were holding him back. He had to turn loose of some things that were hindering him from his spiritual destiny.

All of us have to be willing to cross that threshold.

We must be willing to let God remove from our lives all the compromise, self-justification, and arrogance that may be hindering us from walking in His favor and speaking with His authority.

We must be willing to let Him take the "junk" out of our lives so He can place His own life and His own power within us.

We need to have some spiritual "GUTS" (Giving Up The Stuff).

But once we're equipped with the necessary tools for spiritual success, and we're armed with the weapons we'll need to engage in spiritual warfare, there's only one remaining step for each of us.

That's to prepare ourselves for battle.

CHAPTER 37

BE PREPARED

The official motto of the Boy Scouts of America, "Be Prepared" is actually an awesome philosophy for anyone. To be successful in any endeavor, a person must be prepared.

I'm addicted to sports. I played a ton of sports growing up—football, baseball, basketball, as well as watching the X Games, Motocross and, of course, short track racing. But here's something I know about athletic competition: Whether you're an Olympic gymnast preparing to attack the parallel bars by yourself or the member of a professional football team taking the field with your teammates, you're entering the arena of competition with one vital element:

A plan.

No professional athlete goes into battle without some sort of game plan. In other words, he doesn't just "hope" that things will work out, and he doesn't just rely on his skills and experience to take him to victory.

Even a stock car driver goes into a race with an idea of how he wants to run that race and what he intends to do to win. Of course, in sports, nothing ever happens exactly the way you plan it, so your plans have to be flexible. They have to be adaptable to the changing circumstances around you. But whether you're launching a multi-billion-dollar space probe to Mars or a new doughnut shop in downtown Seattle, you have to begin with a plan.

You have to prepare.

You also have to prepare to represent Christ if you intend to succeed. You must have a plan, a strategy.

So I want to conclude this section on strategic planning by showing you how one of the most successful witnesses for Christ in history approached the task of living *The Revved Life*. Of course, I'm once again referring to Philip, first introduced to us in Acts 6:5. His strategy can be found in Acts 8:5-40.

Philip had this awesome six-step approach. And even though most of these steps flow from common sense, they also convey spiritual wisdom.

So let's briefly analyze Philip's proven method of witnessing and sharing Jesus Christ; the method that's offered to us in God's Word as an effective strategy for leading unbelievers to Christ.

METHOD #1: PHILIP WENT WHERE THE PEOPLE WERE

He didn't wait for the people to come running to him. Let me repeat this strategy for those who may be afraid to leave their comfy warm church pews:

Philip went where the people were.

He *did not wait* for the people to come to him.

In the Acts 8:5 verse that introduces him and his ministry, we are told, "Philip went down to a city in Samaria and proclaimed Christ to the people there." So this is the Bible's simple introduction to this great man. And this means that Philip was the very first person to leave the comforts of Jerusalem and actually *obey* the Lord by taking the Gospel outside the city.

Philip refused to stay in Jerusalem any longer. Motivated partially by the persecution that had commenced in the city (see Acts 8:1) and partially by his own zeal, he chose to break out of the confines of his familiar religious community and to go where he could find lost souls.

Man oh man, I wish the believers of today could follow in the footsteps of Philip!

We're so comfortable in our churches and in our own social circles. We enjoy our Christian music, our Christian movies, and our Christian friends. And I mean, there's nothing wrong with these things! I don't want to slam these worthwhile pursuits.

But I do want to encourage all believers to leave their comfort zones occasionally and to go where they can find people who *do not* know the Lord.

We can't wait for these people to come to us—because they will *never* come to us.

We have to meet people where they are.

We have to seek them out.

And that was Philip's initial strategy. His first strategy was to go where he could find unbelievers.

Jesus told His followers that He wanted them to become "fishers of men" (Matthew 4:19, KJV). But the last time I checked, you have to go where the fish live, if you want to catch fish. I can sit in my La-Z-Boy recliner all day long and wait for the fish to come swimming up to me. I can read books on fishing and buy all the latest gear. I can go to fishing conferences and seminars until I know everything about the art of fishing. I can pray and ask God to make me a great fisherman, and I can binge-watch every show on the Fishing Channel. But until I set my alarm, grab my tackle box, and go drop my hook in the water somewhere, guess what?

I will never catch a fish.

But the deeper I get into my new hobby, the more I'll want to learn about the finer things of fishing. I'll want to become a better fisherman.

Of course, I won't even know what I need to know until I actually start doing some fishing. So the first step to becoming a great fisherman is to simply wake up, put on my boots, get my butt in the boat, and go fishing.

Philip was a great witness for Jesus, not because he was particularly effective, but because God found him at the fishing hole when He was looking for somebody to use. In fact, Philip was so "raw" when he went to Samaria to preach, he didn't know squat about what to do when revival broke out.

He had to call in the "big dogs," Peter and John, to help him.

But eventually, Philip learned what he needed to know by simply doing what he already knew to do.

He was faithful with little, so God entrusted him with greater things (see Luke 6:10).

I've caught a lot of flak from Christians because I dared to leave the sanctity of my pulpit and venture into the world of NASCAR™. Yet these same Christians expect me to be an effective Christ-follower.

In fact, some of them will be the first to tell you that the church pays me to reach people for Christ.

They'll say, "Jeff, you're a pastor. It's your job to reach people far from God!"

That's completely bogus!

That's false.

First of all, I'm not paid by the church to reach people for Jesus; I'm paid to teach *God's people* to reach people for Jesus. I reach people for Jesus because Jesus told me to.

But in addition to that, I can't win a single person without going to the places where people far from God hang out. Jesus went to the places where He could find people who needed God.

And He looks with favor on my efforts to do the same.

"But Jeff!" I often hear. "Those people are bizarre! They're dirty, they're rude, they're crude, they're selfish, and they use foul language. Oh, and they drink too much, too." Yeah, I hear that a lot. These are the literal push-backs many mainstream Christ-followers have said to me over the years.

Another classic statement I hear about going to where people far from God hang out, "I'm just not sure I'd be able to remain pure in an environment like that. Are you sure you are able to maintain your Christianity while associating with people far from God?" My response, blank stare.

Here's the tough truth.

Most Christians don't care about going.

Too many Christians are waiting in their church pews for perfected people to just walk into their churches and sit down beside them.

Seriously!

They're waiting for people who are already cleansed from all guilt and shame to respond to the advertisement on the church sign, to pull their shiny clean cars into the church parking lot, and start attending services. Then they expect these people to get wholeheartedly involved in the life and the work of the church.

Seriously, dude?

What planet do these kind of Christians come from?

That's not the way the world works.

First, you have to catch the fish: reach people through witnessing all you've seen and heard about Jesus.

Then you have to clean the fish: help people get free of the guilt, shame, and ridicule from a life lived outside of knowing Jesus.

But in order to *catch* the fish, you have to go where you can *find* the fish.

And do you know the best place to find fish?

It's *in the water!*—and the best place to fish for people who need Jesus Christ and His salvation: in the waters *outside the church.*

METHOD #2: PHILIP LISTENED FOR AND OBEYED THE LEADING OF GOD

Philip obeyed the leading of the Lord. When God was looking for a man to use in a mighty way, He sent an angel to Philip. Why? Because Philip was already busy witnessing!

Philip was already doing his best to obey the Great Commission.

When God wants to do something new, He always looks for a busy person. He doesn't enlist the aid of somebody who is sitting in the safety of his church or the security of his own home, waiting for the perfect scenario to present itself.

When God needs a champion, God looks for a person who is already involved in the work of the Kingdom. He looks for a person who is already accustomed to responding to the leading of the Lord.

Philip was obedient enough to leave Jerusalem and brave enough to take the Gospel into unfamiliar territory. So God chose Philip when He wanted to do even greater things. The angel told Philip to get in his proverbial car, and travel south on the desert highway that leads from Jerusalem to Gaza. Philip was way up in Samaria at the time. Jerusalem was far to the south, and Gaza was even farther to the south. Nevertheless, Philip obeyed the Lord. He wasn't afraid to venture into new territories to represent Christ.

You too—if you want to be a great witness for Jesus—must learn to listen to God's voice and then obey Him.

You must learn to recognize the leading of the Lord in your life as your experiences teach you to differentiate between God's voice and your own internal self-talk.

But if you'll show yourself willing to obey, God will teach you what you need to know. And He will always let you know where to go and where not to go, when to speak and when to keep silent, when to act and when to wait upon Him.

But after Philip ventured outside his comfort zone to those places where he could find lost souls and after he learned to respond obediently to God's guidance, he learned the importance of approaching people with tact—that was Philip's third strategy.

METHOD #3: PHILLIP APPROACHED PEOPLE WITH TACT

In fact, in Acts 8:26-40, we read the detailed account of how Philip successfully converted the Ethiopian eunuch. This is the Bible's first recorded illustration of a one-on-one presentation of the Gospel, and Philip was the instrument God used to lead this important foreign official to Christ. In this account, we notice that Philip initiated this conversation with the Ethiopian by approaching him cautiously, respectfully, and tactfully.

Philip again listened for the voice of the Lord within his heart.

He sought God's direction in the situation.

And the Spirit of God told Philip, "Go to that chariot and stay near it" (Acts 8:29, NIV).

That's all! Just loiter.

He didn't tell Philip what to do, or say. And He certainly didn't nudge Philip to start preaching or passing out religious tracts on street corners. God simply directed Philip to go near the official's chariot and stay there.

So Philip did as God directed, and soon noticed that the Ethiopian was reading from the book of Isaiah while he was riding in his chariot. And that became Philip's opening. That became Philip's point of contact to initiate a productive and non-threatening conversation with this complete stranger.

If you want to be an effective witness for the Lord, let me give you a tip.

Ready?

Get out of your house.

Out of your church.

Out of your pew.

Out of your comfort zone.

And go where you can find people far from God.

But don't go there to hand out tracts or preach with a megaphone.

Go there to plant yourself.

Get a job somewhere and build relationships. Join an organization and become an active participant. Do something to get near the people you want to win, and do something to become part of their everyday lives so you can earn their trust and establish a platform from which to speak into their lives.

Then do one more thing.

Wait.

Just keep serving the Lord and wait. Your life will be your greatest testimony and confirmation as a credible representative of Christ. And eventually, that moment will come. It's the nature of life. Sooner or later, the person working in the cubicle beside you will do something or say something to open a door for you to naturally share the Gospel as you apply it to their situation.

God gave Philip an opening to witness to the Ethiopian eunuch, and He will give you openings to witness to those within your own sphere of influence.

But God won't pinch you when that moment presents itself. He won't hammer you over the head. And He won't grab your tongue and start wagging it for you.

You will have to use a little bit of wisdom and a little bit of discernment as you look for those opportunities to speak for the Lord.

To speak too soon is to get ahead of God and turn people off; to speak too late is to miss that particular opportunity. But don't worry. If you mess up, God will give you other chances. Just keep bearing witness to the Lord by living for Him.

And just keep praying for the people God places in your life.

But when the time comes, approach cautiously, approach gently, and approach tactfully. Let the person open the door of his heart to you; don't kick the door down and force your way in like you're on God's SWAT team.

The fourth thing Philip did was this: he established common ground with the Ethiopian. He searched for the open door, and then he entered the open door by taking advantage of the common ground that they shared.

METHOD #4: PHILIP ESTABLISHED COMMON GROUND WITH THE ETHIOPIAN

This is a good practice to emulate in your own life.

Just think about it! If a stranger knocks on your front door and you open the door to greet him, his first obligation is to put you at ease by identifying himself and explaining his reason for being there.

His goal should be to remove all fear and intimidation, and make you feel safe so you'll allow him to speak to you or perhaps even enter your home.

The same thing is true spiritually.

When someone knocks on the door of another man's heart, requesting entry, the first obligation of the man seeking entry is to establish the fact that he means no harm.

And the best way to establish this fact is to eliminate fear and create communication by immediately connecting oneself with the unbeliever through a shared experience. In Philip's case, it was the book of Isaiah. It became Philip's "common ground" with the Ethiopian. It became Philip's point of contact and point of entry into the man's life.

God directed Philip to go where he went. But God placed all the rest of the responsibility on Philip.

God left it to Philip to position himself among the people who needed to hear the Gospel.

God left it to Philip to figure out how to approach people.

God left it to Philip to figure out how to establish a point of contact with each person.

And God will leave most of those decisions to you, too. He'll anoint you with His power, and He'll lead you to those people who need to hear what you have to say. But God will leave it to you to figure out when to speak.

And how to start the conversation.

And what to say.

The Great Commission is a joint venture between God and man.

METHOD #5: PHILIP USED THE WORD OF GOD TO PROCLAIM JESUS

Philip used the Word of God to proclaim Jesus. And eventually, you must do the same if you intend to lead people to Christ. As a witness for the Lord, you don't need to shove God's Word down people's throats. You don't need to carry a 10-pound leather Bible under your arm whenever you talk to people about the Lord. And you don't need to leave tracts in restaurants or stand outside baseball stadiums telling the passersby they are going to Hell if they don't repent.

But once you establish a point of contact with a person, you do need to guide the conversation, gently and skillfully, toward those things that God has said about that person's immediate need.

The object of witnessing is to show people that God is the answer to their problems. That He has a solution for their problems. And the solution to all problems begins with a person's spiritual restoration to God.

Once again, God is not going to do this part for you. If you want to be effective, you're going to have to build a reservoir of spiritual knowledge in your own heart and mind that the Holy Spirit can use when you find yourself locked in spiritual warfare for the eternal destiny of another person's soul.

Think of it like this: If you're in a literal battle on a battlefield, you're going to need ammunition to win that battle. But if you wait until the battle begins to think about ammunition, well it'll be too late.

To win the battle, you must prepare for the battle in advance.

Before the battle even begins, you need to stock your supplies.

Fortify your position.

Build up your reserves of food, water, and ammo.

These things need to be at your fingertips so you can quickly put your hands on them in the heat of combat.

And that's precisely the way it is with the Word of God.

In spiritual warfare, the Word of God is our only weapon. It's the sword that we use to fight falsehood and misconception (see Ephesians 6:17). Therefore, before the battle even begins, a Christian must become adept at using his "sword," and he must be able to reach for it in full confidence when the moment of conflict arrives.

So the Christian warrior must have a basic understanding of the Word of God and must memorize a few key Scriptures in order to explain God's plan of salvation and refute the common objections that people raise to the Gospel.

He must be prepared to tell his story.

METHOD #6: PHILIP TOLD HIS STORY

Philip "began with that very passage of Scripture (Isaiah) and told him the good news about Jesus" (Acts 8:35, NIV parentheses mine). Not only did Philip talk to the Ethiopian about the passage of Scripture he had been reading in the book of Isaiah, but Philip went further. He used this passage of Scripture as his launching pad for presenting Christ and God's plan of salvation.

So Philip elaborated on the passage from Isaiah. He told the Ethiopian how this passage applied to his own life, and how this same passage could apply to the Ethiopian's life. Philip told him about the things that recently transpired in Jerusalem, and how Christ changed him and changed the lives of many others.

When you share Christ with a person who doesn't know Him, three things are key:

1. It's essential that you look for an opening to establish common ground.
2. It's essential that you weave the Scriptures into your conversation.
3. It's essential that you personalize what you say by sharing your own story and showing the unbeliever how the Gospel can impact his life, too.

Philip did all these things, and this artful, simple presentation of the Gospel caused the Ethiopian to pull his carriage to the side of the road and go down into a nearby body of water to be baptized by Philip (see Acts 8:36-38).

Nothing is more powerful or more effective than the "show and tell" approach to witnessing that I offered earlier in this book.

Show them the Scriptures.

Then tell them about the good things God has done in your life.

By combining the written Word with your own personal story, you build the confidence that's necessary for someone to achieve saving faith.

The written Word is powerful in its own right. But a personal story of how God's Word has worked for you can be that little push that helps an unbeliever over the hump.

CHAPTER 38

PURSUE A DECISION

Can you remember the day you gave your life to the Lord?

Can you recall how wonderful it felt to be cleansed from all your sin and have the presence of God flood your heart and soul?

Even though salvation has nothing to do with feelings, the feelings are wonderful nonetheless. In fact, there's nothing to compare with the feelings a person experiences when he allows Jesus to enter his heart

But if you liked the feelings you had when you got saved, let me encourage you toward living *The Revved Life*, because the next best thing to salvation is the feeling you get when you actually pray for the first time with someone who's inviting Christ into his heart.

The ultimate goal of witnessing is to lead a person to this decisive act.

The person is then free to give expression to the faith that has been created in his heart.

Without action, the belief in the person's heart will have little effect on his life.

And it won't really count in eternity.

The guy who asks a girl out on a date hasn't sealed the deal until he gets an answer. The guy who asks a girl to marry him or asks a girl's father for permission to marry her hasn't sealed the deal until he gets a response. And similarly, you haven't "sealed the deal" with the person you have been talking to until that person makes a firm decision to turn his life over to Christ.

Jesus would often require people to confess the things they held true in their hearts.

Toward the end of His earthly life, after He performed countless miracles and offered innumerable teachings, Jesus finally found an isolated spot where He had a heart-to-heart conversation with His twelve disciples. In Caesarea Philippi, far removed from the hustle and bustle of Jerusalem and the cities around the Sea of Galilee, Jesus asked his disciples, "Who do people say the Son of Man is?" (Matthew 16:13, NIV).

And the disciples answered Him. They told Jesus that some people viewed Him as John the Baptist, raised from the dead.

Others likened Him to Elijah, Jeremiah, or one of the prophets.

But Jesus didn't instigate this conversation just for the sake of playing a guessing game. From the very beginning, Jesus was leading His disciples somewhere specific.

He was leading them to a decision—and you need to do the same whenever you share Christ with someone.

"But what about you?" Jesus asked his disciples. "Who do you say I Am?" (Matthew 16:15, NIV).

Jesus was looking for a confession.

He was looking for a life-changing moment that would force His disciples to step out of the realm of speculation and finally take a stand for what they believed.

And this is the object of ministry—all ministry. Sharing the plan of salvation is important and praying for lost souls is important. Reading books about evangelism is important and studying the Scriptures is important. But until the person who watches your life and hears your words does something to act on the words you speak, your ministry has produced no fruit.

You haven't yet sealed the deal.

Before a football team takes the field, the members of that team understand their objective. They're going out there to bust heads and win the game.

And before an army enters the field of combat, the soldiers understand their objective. Their objective is to complete the mission.

You, too, need to know your objective before you open your mouth to speak.

You are there to lead that person to a decision.

You are there to lead that person to pray the prayer of repentance and faith with you.

You are there to lead that person to church on Wednesday night or Sunday morning.

You are there to lead that person to your weekly Bible study group or to one of your church's small groups.

You are there to do something to extract a decision—any decision—from the person with whom you speak.

And if you know your objective, that internal knowledge will guide you in everything you say during your conversation.

You can lead a horse to water, but unless the horse drinks, he will remain thirsty. You can lead a child to school, but unless the child learns and unless he demonstrates what he's learned by taking and passing a test, your trip to school is unproductive.

You must lead that person through the Scriptures so he can finally "see" what he has never seen before—

That God loves him.

That God has a plan for his life.

And that God has a solution for his problems.

But unless the person takes a conscious step to respond to the offer of salvation, all this newfound understanding will be wasted.

The Ethiopian acted on Philip's presentation of the Gospel. He "went down into the water and Philip baptized him" (Acts 8:38, NIV). So Philip's ultimate goal was not a stimulating conversation; Philip's ultimate goal was a decisive act of faith. And that explains his strategy.

From the very beginning, when God led Philip to Samaria to share the Gospel with people outside Jerusalem, Philip knew what he was there to do and he knew why he was there to do it.

But he also knew *how* to do what God appointed him to do. He knew how to approach people, penetrate their carefully erected defenses, and lead them to a life-changing moment of decision that would forever alter their lives and their eternal destinies.

You must do the same.

Equipped with the wisdom of God, the wisdom of God's Word, the wisdom of experience, and a basic understanding of human nature and human needs, you should obey the leading of the Lord in your life and go where you can find the people who need Christ.

When you're successful, there will be rejoicing in Heaven over the salvation of a lost soul. And there will be an incredible sense of satisfaction in your own soul as another person is won for Christ and another life is placed on the road to restoration.

So seek.

Pursue.

Act.

Share.

Seal the deal.

And God's future rewards will await you.

FINAL ACT: VICTORY

SO GET GOING.
You're gassed up for the journey.
You've got your road map.
The road ahead is clear.
God doesn't make mistakes.
He knows what He's doing.
Everything He's ever done in your life has an eternal purpose.
A redemptive rationale.

Your job is to realize it.
Discover it.
Embrace it.
And then figure out how to use it to bring glory to Him.

The world is waiting.
Stop looking over your shoulder.
Stop wondering if you are enough.
Turn off the critics.

Stop worrying ...
And reach people.
It's time for you to get going.

Remember, victory is not up to you.
This whole process of reaching people.
Or getting someone "saved."
Or leading someone to Christ.
Or being important while doing it.
It's really not your deal.

This whole notion about finding your uniqueness.
Discovering your specific design.
It's really overrated if you don't show up.
Winning starts when you do the work.
Your job is to show up.
Daily.

It's time to start
You'll be amazed at how impactful life can be.
How persuasive your story is, when you share it.
When you live.
When you stay in your chosen place of spiritual service.
God will be faithful to you.

THE REVVED LIFE within you is coming alive.

I am but one bold voice. NO longer silent.
There is another within you.
It's up to you to bring it out.

I hope you will.

ABOUT THE AUTHOR

Jeff Knight is the lead pastor of The Rock Church, a large and innovative family of believers in Monroe, Washington. But pastoral ministry is Jeff's "day" job. His other passion in life is stock car racing. In fact, Jeff is a NASCAR™ driver.

Jeff and his wife, Melinda, became the lead pastors of "The Rock" in 2000 when his parents were tragically killed in a plane crash off the coast of California while returning from a missionary trip to Mexico. Joe and Linda Knight had established The Rock Church when Jeff was just a boy. But as the church grew under Joe and Linda's guidance, Jeff also grew in the knowledge and the favor of God. And under tragic circumstances, Jeff assumed responsibility for the church shortly after his parents' death.

In his personal life, in his ministry, and on the racetrack, Jeff lives "full throttle" and he lives to win. He strives to achieve every goal God has set before him, and he tries to impact as many lives as possible while pursuing the prize. This explains why Jeff leaves his pastoral study every weekend to get his hands dirty in the real world. This explains why he leaves the familiarity of his church environment to purposely place himself within a subculture of people who are often removed from faith, yet who need the love of God.

Through the way he lives, the way he wins, the way he conducts himself within the racing world, and even the way he loses, Jeff is winning hearts and changing lives while steering people to the Lord and to his church. And through the way he presents the Gospel when the opportunity arises, Jeff is reaching people too, and building a congregation of others who do the same. In fact, The Rock is a life-change factory and a fast-paced school of personal discipleship.

Along with his wife, Melinda, and his daughter, Seven Addison, Jeff is showing his congregants how to live triumphantly and with God's favor in every aspect of their lives. Conducting himself as an unabashed representative of Christ while on the racetrack, Jeff is commanding the respect of those inside and outside his church who formerly questioned his "double" lifestyle. By winning at ministry, Jeff is reproducing his own talents hundreds of times over in others. And by winning at life, Jeff is drawing individuals to Christ and influencing both his community and a subculture of American life that few believers can affect. Jeff Knight is living *The Revved Life.*

CONTACT JEFF KNIGHT
To get information about *The Revved Life* and
additional resources available from Jeff Knight, visit:
Jeffknight.com

Jeff speaks weekly at The Rock Church on a variety of Christian
based subjects with relevancy to life's challenges.
To view them and more, visit:
TheRockChurch.info

He is also available for guest appearances to
deliver a keynote, half-day, or full-day version of this content,
depending on your needs. If you are interested in finding
out more, please visit his Speaking page at:
JeffKnight.com/speaking

You can also connect with Jeff (aka Knightrous) here:
Blog: *JeffKnight.com*
Facebook: *facebook.com/JeffKnightcom*
Twitter: *twitter.com/Knightrous*
LinkedIn: *linkedin.com/in/JeffRKnight*

REDEMPTION
PRESS

To order additional copies of this book, please visit
www.redemption-press.com.
Also available on Amazon.com and BarnesandNoble.com
Or by calling toll free 1-844-2REDEEM.

CPSIA information can be obtained at www.ICGtesting.com
Printed in the USA
BVOW02s2252030615

402773BV00003B/3/P